[RIOT]

....

[RIOT]

....

Walter Dean Myers

SCHOLASTIC INC.

New York Toronto London Auckland
Sydney New Delhi Hong Kong

Photo insert design by Arlene Goldberg.
Cover design by Michael Nagin.

Copyright © 2009 by Walter Dean Myers.
All rights reserved. Published by Scholastic Inc., 557 Broadway, New York, NY 10012,
by arrangement with Egmont USA.
Printed in the U.S.A.

ISBN-13: 978-0-545-26415-0
ISBN-10: 0-545-26415-4

13 14 15   40   22 21

[To Jackie Monahan O'Brien]

[Contents]

[CAST OF CHARACTERS]

CLAIRE JOHNSON, 15, very pretty

PRISCILLA SKINNER, 15, her friend,
dark skin, pretty

ELLEN JOHNSON, 37, her mother

ROBERT VAN VORST, 15, her friend,
slightly overweight but handsome

LIAM, 17, an employee of the Johnsons'

MAEVE, 16, Liam's fiancée

DENNIS RILEY, 17, member of the Dead
Rabbits gang

TOMMY ENRIGHT, 19, member of the Dead
Rabbits gang

BILLY EVANS, 12

OFFICER MCCLUSKER, 26, police officer

OFFICER BARNES, 29, police officer

JOHN ANDREWS, 41, a Southerner

JOHN JOHNSON, 40, Claire's father

ROSIE LYONS, 14, a friend of Maeve's

WALT WHITMAN, 44, poet

FARLEY, 11, Whitman's servant

PRIVATE KELLY, 25, Union soldier

PRIVATE PARKER, 24, Union soldier

PRIVATE JOSHUA LANCASTER, 17, Union soldier

GRIFFIN, 15

CHARLES HICKEY, 28, police officer

KELLY, 19

MARY POOLE, 15

JOHNNY, 15

CAPTAIN ROBERTS, 32, Union army officer

MARGARET ADDAMS, 32, Matron of the
Colored Orphan asylum

CAITLIN DONAHUE, 16

THE REVEREND CURRY, 46, pastor of a
Baptist Church

[RIOT]

....

[FADE IN]

EXT. NEW YORK CITY—JULY, PRESENT DAY

AERIAL SHOT. As the camera zooms in, we see the
city below, with its skyscrapers jutting boldly into the
sky high above the street-level chaos. As the camera
comes closer, we see the blur of vehicles in the city
streets.

The camera comes even lower, and we see rapidly
moving traffic. The streets of Lower Manhattan
are glutted with cars. We see pedestrians darting
in between the cars and hear the blare of a hip-hop
recording that matches the frantic pace of the traffic.

The camera zooms in even farther and focuses on a
YOUNG WOMAN eating lunch on the white steps of a
building. She is on her cell phone as the camera begins
to zoom out, and we see the city as a rich mosaic of
colors, which turns into an urban gray blur. The blur
lasts for a few seconds.

EXT. NEW YORK CITY—MAY 1954

AERIAL SHOT, then zoom in. This time the buildings are not as stark, the traffic in the streets not quite so frantic. The cars are older. The camera focuses on a MAN eating lunch on a park bench. The newspaper he is reading has a headline about the Supreme Court's decision in Brown v. the Topeka Board of Education. We see the date: it is 1954.

A YOUNG WHITE COUPLE is sitting down not far from the MAN reading the paper. The young man puts his hand on her knee, and she pushes it quickly away. We see her stand and start to walk away as the camera begins to zoom out. She turns to see if he is following as the shot becomes more distant and blurs.

EXT. NEW YORK CITY—JULY 1900

AERIAL SHOT, then zoom in again. The streets of Lower Manhattan are still clogged, but this time with horse-drawn carriages. Men in bowler hats chat amiably on one corner. On another corner two NEWSBOYS, one white and one black, fight as other boys cheer them on. The camera focuses on a YOUNG WHITE MAN reading an illustrated paper as he leans against a lamppost.

The camera pans away from the YOUNG MAN and

onto a crowded street on which we see pushcarts and
Jewish vendors. Here we see a YOUNG BLACK GIRL
feeding bread crumbs to pigeons. She tries to shoo away
a larger pigeon. It refuses to move, and she stamps her
foot, sending the small covey of birds into the air as the
camera zooms out again to a blurred view of the area.

EXT. NEW YORK CITY—JULY 11, 1863

AERIAL SHOT, then the sound of music rises as the
camera slowly moves in once again. The streets of Lower
Manhattan are indistinct but sharpen gradually. We
hear the clicking of telegraph keys, and words appear on
the screen, moving from right to left:

> July 11, 1863. Generals optimistic after
> Gettysburg. Losses heavy. Lincoln urged
> to call up more men.

Behind the words, we see the streets. There is a brief stop
on a row of crudely built wooden dwellings. We see a
heavy WOMAN selling fish on the streets and a YOUNG
MAN getting a haircut from a sidewalk BARBER.

The camera pans past several streets, on one of which a
number of YOUNG WHITE PEOPLE are arguing. Their
dress is poor, the men in patched pants and ill-fitting
shirts, the women in shabby long dresses, some with
dirty aprons over them. The camera pans past, then

stops and returns to the activity for a long moment.

EXT. FIVE POINTS AREA—SAME DAY (CONTINUOUS)

> FIRST YOUNG WOMAN
> From the way the papers are reading, I
> thought the bloody war was almost over.
> What do they need a draft for? Stealing
> our young men away for nothing.

> SECOND YOUNG WOMAN
> As long as they're keeping it far away from
> Henry Street, they can do with it what they
> want is what I'm saying. The good Lord
> has his face turned away from the likes of
> us, and that's for sure.

> FIRST YOUNG WOMAN
> Johnny McCall was down at the office
> where the government men pulled the
> names out of a drum. He said you would
> have thought they were pulling the
> names of the first men to waltz their way
> through the pearly gates, what with all the
> speeches and the chests sticking out. He
> said the firemen are hopping mad. Can
> you imagine the firemen having to leave to
> fight a war when we need them right here?

                    SECOND YOUNG WOMAN
          Well, if I was a man, it would be over me
          dead body they'd be reaching for their tea!
          Imagine, poor men leaving their wives and
          homes to go fight while the rich men pat
          their bellies and wave them off with their
          silk hankies!

                     FIRST YOUNG WOMAN
          Ay! And you can bet your sweet life on
          that, too.

The camera moves on, and we see a NEWSBOY selling
a paper to a wounded SOLDIER. The SOLDIER is tall,
gaunt. He carries a bundle stuck in his crutch. He looks
up toward the camera and then quickly away.

INT. THE PEACOCK INN—JULY 13, 1863

The Peacock Inn is a shabby-genteel restaurant-tavern
on Bedford Street, run by JOHN and ELLEN JOHNSON,
who live upstairs with their daughter, CLAIRE.

CLAIRE JOHNSON (15) and her best friend,
PRISCILLA SKINNER (also 15), are sitting at one of
the rectangular tables. They are sewing a quilt.

CLAIRE is thin and pretty, with skin color light enough

to pass for Caucasian. She has soft brown eyes, sharp
features, and chestnut-colored hair, which she has
combed up until it almost forms a halo around a sweet
face. She is wearing a flower-patterned cotton dress
and a neat apron.

PRISCILLA is dark, obviously African American, and
is dressed similarly. She is also pretty, with a round face
that is quick to smile.

PRISCILLA
So, if you were feeling sick, would you let
a doctor examine you?

CLAIRE
Are you feeling sick?

PRISCILLA
No, I was just wondering. What would you
do if he asked you to undress?

CLAIRE
I'd do it—as long as he had his eyes closed
and his hands behind his back and he was
at least a hundred and twelve! And you?

PRISCILLA
I'd faint dead away, and then he could do
whatever he wanted to me.

CLAIRE

Priscilla!

ELLEN JOHNSON (37), CLAIRE's mother, enters
with a mop and bucket. She looks somewhat older
than her age but is attractive, and the resemblance
between her daughter and her is clear.

ELLEN

And what are you girls up to?

CLAIRE

Priscilla's got her squares wrong. I'm
straightening them out for her.

PRISCILLA

They aren't wrong, Mrs. Johnson, just
different from what Claire had in mind.
You know how bossy she can be.

ELLEN

(looking at the quilt)
So what did you have in mind?

CLAIRE

Priscilla was telling me how the slaves
make quilts in the South that are really
like maps. They have a star and paths that
lead to the star.

ELLEN
(looking at PRISCILLA)
Priscilla, you were born in Brooklyn. How
do you know about what the poor slaves
are doing?

PRISCILLA
From my great-aunt Esther. She was born
in Virginia. When the man who owned
her died, her father ran off north with the
whole family.

ELLEN
This the old woman who lives uptown in
Broadway Alley?

PRISCILLA
Yes.

ELLEN
Sweet lady, she is. I don't think the
rowdies will get that far uptown.

ROBERT VAN VORST (15) enters. He is white
and slightly overweight but handsome and well
dressed, with dark hair combed straight back
and a high forehead.

ELLEN

Are we having a convention? Everyone's
here!

ROBERT

I've just been down to the Grand Street
draft office, inquiring whether I might
apply for a commission. They obviously
need good men, and I'm willing to go.

CLAIRE

I heard they were rioting near the
waterfront.

ROBERT

Slackers. They're actually protesting
against the draft! Can you believe it?
Father said that there was a police lineup
across from the *Tribune*. They've thrown
rocks through the windows of the stores
along the side streets.

ELLEN

It's not safe to be out and about. John says
they were ugly this morning. He said the
Dead Rabbits were running around as if
they owned the streets.

ROBERT

Well, then, the army will just have to deal
with gangs like the Dead Rabbits, won't
they? They're mostly young drunks and old
people, anyway. If I were commanding a
battalion, I'd send a half dozen of my best
men to put down the gangs.

ELLEN

Robert, they're not having fifteen-year-
olds commanding battalions.

PRISCILLA

I think they could, because you just have
to tell the men where to go and what to do.

CLAIRE

You think they could because it's your
precious Robert who wants to lead them,
Priscilla. Too bad he's not a doctor.

PRISCILLA

Claire Johnson!

ROBERT

(full of himself)

She's right, of course. Officers lead men
and direct them to where they need to
go. Like Meade at Gettysburg. Did you

read in the *Times* how his men held their
positions against Longstreet?

PRISCILLA
What time is it? I have to get to the
orphanage.

CLAIRE
Robert, you're not carrying Priscilla's
books today. Do you think it's really safe?
I mean, they're throwing rocks. . . .

ROBERT
I'll go with her to see she's safe.

CLAIRE
(teasing)
        And don't forget to put your arm around her
        if you see any danger, Captain Van Vorst.

PRISCILLA
(gathering her reticule)
        Claire!

CLAIRE
(serious)
        Both of you keep your eyes open!

ROBERT and PRISCILLA are at the door of the Peacock.

> PRISCILLA

Ta-ta, Lady Claire.

> CLAIRE

Ta-ta, my dear.

ROBERT and PRISCILLA exit. CLAIRE starts to put away the sewing.

> ELLEN

Do you think Priscilla's really sweet on Robert?

> CLAIRE

She'd marry him tomorrow if she could get him from under his mother's thumb.

> ELLEN

A man that's under his mother's thumb needs to stay there until he can wiggle out himself.

> CLAIRE

Priscilla's ready to give him a tug. She thinks his mother doesn't want to let him grow up. Like all mothers.

> ELLEN

Nonsense. I can't wait until you've hopped

from the branch and tried your own wings.

CLAIRE

And you're supposed to be teaching
me the rest of the song about the black
rosebud. Did you forget that?

ELLEN

And you have a sweet voice. I'd tell Mum
that if she were still alive. It's the Irish in
your heart that makes your voice so sweet.
Let's hear you sing.

CLAIRE

(singing)
The Erne at its highest flood,
I dashed across unseen,
For there was lightning in my blood,
My dark Rosaleen!
My own Rosaleen!
Oh, there was lightning in my blood,
My dark Rosaleen!

ELLEN

Oh, and you do have such a sweet voice.
If your feet weren't so big, I could marry
you off before the weekend!
(kisses CLAIRE's hand)

CLAIRE
Ma, why is this girl coming this
afternoon?

ELLEN
Liam's friend? Because I can't do all the
cooking and cleaning and everything
that's to be done in this place. You know
that, Claire. And your father wants you
to continue school. Get something beside
daydreams in that pretty head of yours.

CLAIRE
Mother, you know what I mean. . . . If
you're going to hire someone to work in
the Peacock, then why not Priscilla? She
loves the children in the orphanage, but
there's not a lot for her there.

ELLEN
(sits at the table with her daughter)
The Peacock is quite a lovely business,
Claire, and you know it. Your father and I
want to buy it one day. We've been talking
with Mr. Valentine—

CLAIRE
I don't care about Mr. Valentine.

ELLEN

Well, I do, and your father does as well.
We're trying to convince him to sell us
this place. It has a good reputation—

CLAIRE

He's been letting it run down. We're
giving it back its reputation.

ELLEN

And so we are, colleen. This place has
been here for a while and people know
about it. But he wants it to be a place for
a high-class clientele. We don't want to
open some place like the Gallant Frog
down the street, do we? Oh, is that ever a
hooligan haven.

CLAIRE

He means a place for *white* people?

ELLEN

There's nothing wrong with white people,
Claire. And seeing that I am one of them,
I'm hoping that you can understand that.
We'll have all kinds of people here if your
father and I have anything to do with it.

CLAIRE

In two months, this war will be over. Then
there won't be any more slavery and then it
won't matter if any of us are white or black.

ELLEN

Did the Good Lord himself tell you that,
Claire? Because if He did, I'm very much
impressed. The last person I know who
heard the Lord talking back to him was
your great-uncle, and that was only when
he had a few pints in him.

CLAIRE

So we can't hire Priscilla because Mr.
Valentine wants white people working here?

ELLEN

Your father says that once we get the
place going, we can have anyone we want
staying here and working here. Do you
think your father, a black man, would
turn away his own people?

CLAIRE

When we do own this place, I'm going to
have the fanciest lace curtains you've ever
seen. And I saw the absolutely perfect
chandelier in that shop on Broadway. The

moment people walk in the front door,
they'll know they're in a place of quality.
But—and this is important—I'll have
different sets of curtains for different days.
Some gleaming white and others just a little
off white—maybe ivory—with those little
designs that you see in the fancy shops.

ELLEN

Is it an inn you'll be running or a palace?

CLAIRE

It'll be an inn but so fine that people will
come to New York just to visit us. And
we'll steal that sour-faced little cook from
Fraunces Tavern.

ELLEN

You've got your dreams neatly lined up,
haven't you?

CLAIRE

They're better dreams than Mr. Valentine
will ever have and I'll thank you for
knowing that, I will. And now I'll be off to
fetch the milk for this afternoon's tea.

ELLEN

You'll be doing no such thing. There's too

much afoot out there. Your father was
about this morning and he said it's not
just the roughnecks out there. It's a mob
of people and they're in an ugly mood.
They've even torn down some telegraph
poles on the East Side, although I don't
see how that does very much for them.

CLAIRE

Father said they're protesting against the
draft. They don't want to fight in the war.

ELLEN

Well, neither do I, but you don't see me
tearing down any telegraph poles, do you?
All across Fourteenth Street! Of all the
foolishness. We'd better all stay in until
things grow quiet again. And the talk is that
they're attacking black people in the street.

CLAIRE

I don't see why you have to be a black
person or a white person. Why can't you
just be a person?

ELLEN

Well, if you're a rose or a daisy, you're
still a flower. People see what they have a

mind to see. You were born a girl. Do you
have a complaint about that, too?

CLAIRE
(pensive)
I'm not complaining.
When I was born, did you write to your
mother about me?

ELLEN
Of course I did.

CLAIRE
Did you tell her I was black or white?

ELLEN
I told her you were a baby girl and that all
of your parts seemed reasonably intact.
(tries to lighten the conversation)
Let's see, you had one nose, as many toes
as you were needing—

CLAIRE
And did you tell her that my dad is black?

ELLEN
I wrote that he was tall, dark, and quite
the good looker. I let her imagine the rest.

The hard part was skirting around the
notion that he wasn't Catholic.

CLAIRE
Oh, you're sneaky clever, Mrs. Johnson.

There is a knock on the door, and LIAM (17) and
MAEVE (16) enter.

LIAM
Morning, Mrs. Johnson. Morning, Claire.

ELLEN
Morning, Liam. You're looking handsome
today.

CLAIRE
But why are you combing your hair straight
back? You know I never like it that way.

LIAM
My friend thinks it makes me look older.

CLAIRE
(Glances at Maeve)
Does she now?

ELLEN
And does your friend have a name?

MAEVE

It's Maeve, ma'am. And I've been sent by
Father Donahue to see about the job you'd
be having.

ELLEN

Oh, yes. Well, I'm glad the two of you
aren't running around the streets like
madmen. Can you use a cold glass of
lemonade?

LIAM

That I could, ma'am. I was telling Maeve
how I worked here from time to time and
how you were looking for a girl. She's sort
of my intended.

ELLEN

Well, sit yourselves down. Lemonade is as
good sitting as it is standing.
(LIAM and MAEVE sit)

CLAIRE

I didn't know you had an intended, Liam.
And all this time I've had my hopes up.

LIAM

Go on with yourself, Claire.

ELLEN

How old are you to be thinking of
marriage?

LIAM

Old enough if I can keep working steady.
I'm doing errands for you, but I'll shame
the devil and tell you right out that I'm
looking for something stronger.

MAEVE

My mother wasn't but sixteen, same as me,
when she got married.

ELLEN

Well, those were the old days—when you
married coming down the gangplank. So
tell me where you worked before.

MAEVE

For a gentleman who lived on Gramercy
Park. He was an old man who needed
looking after. I cleaned for him and
sometimes made him tea. But he up and
died in a sudden way and left me without
a job and the week's pay because his
daughter said she didn't know if I had
been paid or not.

ELLEN

Which means you don't have references?

MAEVE

No, ma'am. But I go to Mass on a regular
basis and I give to the poor. I was in
church when I seen Father Donahue.

ELLEN

We're looking for someone who's worked
in a hotel.

MAEVE

(looking about)
I can pour pints, too.

ELLEN

Learn that at Mass, did you?

MAEVE

No, ma'am.

CLAIRE

Can you make square corners on a bed?

MAEVE

I don't know. I never tried it. Are you
working here?

ELLEN

When she's not planning visits from the queen.

There is the sound of a disturbance outside, and we
hear shouts and some cursing as a small group passes.

LIAM

(excitedly)

They're headed uptown. I think I'm going
with them.

(gets up to leave)

CLAIRE

Were you drafted?

LIAM

No, but I'm protesting! Miss Ellen, do you
know what life is about in Five Points? It's
not pretty.

ELLEN

I know, but you're such a darling lad.
We'd hate to see you hurt, Liam. Wouldn't
we, Claire?

CLAIRE

(quietly)

He knows that.

LIAM exits.

>   MAEVE
> Oh, he's all excited, he is. They were
> singing about going to Dublin and
> marching as gay as you please all the way
> down Mercer Street. And every time they
> came to the end of a line with a "Whack
> follol de rah" they would break out a
> window!

>   CLAIRE
> That's terrible. Why would anyone want to
> do that?

>   MAEVE
> Well, it's the Irish against the swells and
> the Coloreds. They've been pushing us
> around too long, they have. You can't
> walk down the sidewalk without a swell
> pushing you off into the street or one of
> the Coloreds taking your jobs. I hear they
> have them by the hundreds in Jersey City
> just waiting to rush over to New York at
> the drop of a hat.

> You won't be able to find a scrap of work
> that they won't do for half the money.

That's how the Coloreds are. They'll work
for nothing until they chase us out and
we'll be the beggars and street sweepers.
It's in the Bible!

ELLEN

Well, I'll be! Darling, you won't do for
this job. We need someone with more
experience. I'm very sorry. I'm sure you'll
find a good job somewhere else.

MAEVE

Can I wait here for a moment in case Liam
comes back?

ELLEN
(looks toward CLAIRE)

Well, I have to run to the chemist to pick
up some medicine for Dr. Smith. My
husband works for him.

MAEVE
(sarcastically)

Fancy that.

ELLEN

I'll be back shortly.

ELLEN exits.

MAEVE looks around the Peacock. Where she was apprehensive in dealing with ELLEN, now she begins to look more confident as she glances sideways at CLAIRE.

> MAEVE
> So, do they treat you good here?

> CLAIRE
> That's my ma that runs the place.

> MAEVE
> Then you've got it nice, haven't you?

> CLAIRE
> Nice enough. Do you like breaking windows?

> MAEVE
> It's a way to get back at the swells. They hate to lose money, you know. A swell would rather see his wife die than lose a hundred dollars. That's because they enjoy being a swell more than anything.

> CLAIRE
> Everyone should enjoy being who they are.

MAEVE
Well, we certainly enjoy being Irish, don't we?

CLAIRE
I'm . . . I'm only half Irish.

MAEVE
And what's the other half?

CLAIRE
My father's black.

MAEVE
No!

CLAIRE
Yes!

MAEVE
No!

CLAIRE
Yes!

MAEVE
Does your mother know?

CLAIRE

Of course she does.

MAEVE crosses to CLAIRE and examines her closely,
even touches her hair as CLAIRE sits stiffly.

MAEVE

You'd never know it! And you'd be a fool
to let anyone in on it, wouldn't you?

CLAIRE

Why would I care?

MAEVE

Is that why I didn't get the job? Because of
what I said about the Coloreds?

CLAIRE

My mother wanted someone with
experience.

MAEVE
(leans forward)

I'm not saying that it's wrong to be a
Colored. But I don't want to be one, and I
don't like them. You're not really Colored
no matter what your father is about. You're
as white as me from the looks of you, and

you'd be a fool to be anything else.

CLAIRE

I think you'd better go now.

MAEVE

(somewhat cocky)

You don't look very tough. You ever been
in a fight?

CLAIRE

Do you know how easy it would be for me
to have you arrested?

MAEVE

That's the swell part of you coming out,
isn't it? Only the swells say it with their
noses in the air like the Coloreds.

CLAIRE

You don't make a bit of sense.

MAEVE

If you were regular people like I am, or like
Liam, you would be on my side, wouldn't
you? You wouldn't be threatening to call
the coppers, would you? That's what
they're fighting about in the streets, dearie.
How the Irish are the ones being pushed

around. And how the swells are looking to
send us off to fight for the Coloreds.

ELLEN enters, carrying a small package. She quickly
senses something is going on between the two girls.

                    ELLEN
The order was only half filled. John will
have to get the rest another time.

                    MAEVE
Maybe I'll be back, ma'am, in case you
change your mind.

MAEVE exits.

                    ELLEN
Something going on?

                    CLAIRE
No. No, not really.

EXT. DOWNTOWN NEW YORK—SAME DAY

A CROWD of some fifty young white men and some
women has gathered across the street from the offices
of the Tribune. Some throw stones at the building. The
camera pans the CROWD, stops for a moment on an

excited LIAM, who seems slightly confused as he tries to take in everything around him.

We turn a corner and see DENNIS RILEY (17) and TOMMY ENRIGHT (19), two members of the street gang known as the Dead Rabbits. They are dressed in recently stolen top hats, formal dress pants (also stolen), and suspenders over white undershirts. Both men have red ribbons pinned around the left cuff of their pants. They are talking to a group of eager young boys. Among them is BILLY EVANS (12).

> DENNIS RILEY
> The coppers are waiting for us to make
> a move, but we're biding our time, boys.
> Waiting for the tide to come to us. What
> we're looking for is someone to do some
> carrying. Ya getting a cut of everything ya
> carry and you can take that as gospel.

> TOMMY ENRIGHT
> Ten percent is yours off the top. We do
> the snatching while you hang back on the
> corner. Then we bring you the goods and
> you carry it to where we tell you. We'll deal
> with the coppers. All you need to do is
> watch out for the Bowery Boys, who don't
> have enough tin in their kidneys to do the
> lifting. You kiddies with us or against us?

BILLY EVANS

I'd rather join the army meself. You get
a regular gun and bullets, and they give
you three hundred dollars for your pocket.
You can't beat that, and you don't have to
do no running.

TOMMY ENRIGHT

Wha? Wha? Wha you gonna do, kiddy?
You gonna go off and fight for the darkies?
The rich people are getting to two-step
away from the bloody war for three
hundred dollars. Now figure this one out.
They're selling blacks down in Georgia for
a thousand dollars. That means that your
life ain't even worth half of what a black
man's life is worth. That's what you going
for? Huh? That's what you going for?

BILLY EVANS

I always thought about going into the
army. Maybe the 7th Irish.

DENNIS RILEY

You got your war right here in the streets,
pie-face. And after this little rough-and-
tumble is over, they're going to know we
got something to say and it ain't only the
abolitionists making the newspapers.

BILLY EVANS

I heard the coppers are shooting at people.
They got a guy on Tenth Street and shot
him in both legs!

TOMMY ENRIGHT

That's what they're doing, Billy boy. Don't
you see? They don't really care about none
of this because half the cops are as Irish
as we are. They're shooting up in the air
and down at the ground so they don't hurt
us. And you don't need to be anywhere
near the shooting because all you're going
to be doing is carrying the goods we bring
you. You want to be a Dead Rabbit, or you
want to go join the little girls' brigade? We
can call ya Little Miss Molly.

BILLY EVANS

Yeah, yeah. I'm with you. But this makes
me a full member, right? I get me ten
percent, like you said, and I'm a Rabbit?

DENNIS RILEY

It's a hard bargain you drive, Billy, but
you're never gonna forget this day. This
is the day you woke up a kid and went to
sleep a man. That's right. You're going to
sleep tonight a real man.

BILLY EVANS
(apprehensive)
>We gonna be beating up Coloreds, too? I
>don't like that part.

TOMMY ENRIGHT
>Nah. We got no time for that. That ain't
>smart, and smart is my middle name,
>Bucky Boy. Okay, let's get the boys
>moving. Get them going across the street
>and right toward the shops. Keep a line
>of the biggest guys on the left, nearest the
>coppers, to hold them off. We'll throw a
>little charge at the police at the same time
>we smash the windows. Then it's grab and
>run, a few fists and stones, and everybody
>is out of here. You kids get to that corner
>and be ready when we come back.

The camera looks down the street.

TOMMY ENRIGHT
(cont'd)
>You ready?

BILLY EVANS & FRIENDS
(in unison)
>Ready!

DENNIS RILEY and TOMMY ENRIGHT start across the street, with ENRIGHT leading. The camera pulls back, and we see a knot of young men and women, who start to cheer when they see the two gang members come forward. The CROWD starts to follow the two toward a line of stores.

The camera quickly switches to a group of POLICEMEN, who start toward the CROWD. There is a direct confrontation, and the POLICE begin to beat the members of the CROWD.

CUT TO:
CLOSE-UP of MAEVE. Her face is a picture of incredible anger as she screams at the POLICE.

CUT TO:
MAIN SHOT: We see TOMMY ENRIGHT fall. The camera moves into the conflict, and we are in the middle of it, with bodies flashing around us, as well as cries of pain. There is the sound of a gunshot, and we see POLICE shooting into the air. The camera spins crazily and everything goes dark, but we still hear the sounds of the battle. Then the sounds stop.

POLICE OFFICER
(voice-over)
      That'll show them. Just leave them lying

there. Their relatives can come sort them
out in the morning if they have the mind
to. That'll show them. It's late in the day.
Things should be quieting down a bit.

We see nine POLICE OFFICERS, some winded from
their efforts, looking down the street. The camera pans
down the street, and we see the CROWD in disarray,
with some holding their heads. It has been a brutal
encounter.

EXT. A QUIET SECTION OF FIFTH AVENUE—SAME DAY

We see a street sign that indicates that we are on Fifth
and Fortieth Street. Two UPPER-CLASS MEN and a
WOMAN are walking down the street.

> FIRST UPPER-CLASS MAN
> They'll go home once it gets dark. Maybe
> if they sleep off the liquor, they'll wake
> with some sense in their heads.

> SECOND UPPER-CLASS MAN
> In any case, the mayor will have things under
> control by the morning. I'm sure of that.

> UPPER-CLASS WOMAN
> Are those people coming this way?

We see a small CROWD of people walking along, almost casually—except for the clubs some are carrying.

                    FIRST UPPER-CLASS MAN
The very nerve of these people.

                    UPPER-CLASS WOMAN
We'd better get inside.

                    SECOND UPPER-CLASS MAN
My goodness! What could they want in this neighborhood?

                    FIRST UPPER-CLASS MAN
I don't believe their morals stretch far beyond what they can drink or have the pleasure of stealing. But I agree, better to be indoors.

INT. THE COLORED ORPHAN ASYLUM—SAME DAY

Beside a row of neatly made beds, two WOMEN in their late twenties—one white, one black—and an elderly WHITE MAN are gathering the CHILDREN and lining them up. There is a clear sense of urgency as they get the CHILDREN, all between four and ten, ready to

leave. In the background we hear occasional shouts and
the sound of breaking glass.

We see PRISCILLA cradling a baby in her right arm and
holding the hand of a small black girl.

                    WHITE WOMAN
          Hold hands! Quickly! Quickly! We'll
          march smartly through the side doors!

                    WHITE MAN
          They're breaking the windows!

                    PRISCILLA
          Come along! Come along! This way!

She starts through an open door. The CHILDREN,
obviously distressed, begin to file out. One older girl
stops to straighten the corner of a bed and then her
hand is taken by the WHITE WOMAN.

                    PRISCILLA
          Why would they want to hurt the
          children?

                    WHITE MAN
          We can't reason with them, that's for sure.
          Let's just get out of here.

PRISCILLA
(her face determined)
     Go!

PRISCILLA stands at the doorway while the last of the
CHILDREN are taken out. She looks around the still,
neat room. Her face tightens, and for a moment, it looks
as if she will burst into tears. But then she becomes
strong again and exits.

We hear distinct sounds of glass breaking and a
pounding on the door as the last child leaves. There is
more pounding, and then a young white WOMAN, one
of the rioters, enters. She puts her hands on her hips as
she surveys the scene.

Suddenly, a black BOY pops into the room and runs to
a small desk at the front of the room. He pushes aside a
pile of paper and takes a Bible from the desk, unaware
of the WOMAN's presence. He starts to head for the
door and then freezes as he sees the WOMAN. She
crosses to him and takes the Bible out of his hand. For
a moment they are frozen in time. The noise from the
other room increases as the other rioters draw near.

The WOMAN gives the Bible back to the BOY and
gives him a little push toward the door. As he reaches
the door, PRISCILLA appears in the doorway,
looking for the BOY. The two women look at each

other, and then PRISCILLA and the BOY exit.

A group of RIOTERS enters. The men look in closets
and throw the bedding and clothes they find onto the
floor. The women begin picking it up.

> FIRST WOMAN
> (holding up a child's garment)
>> It's perfect for my Mary.

> SECOND WOMAN
>> Too good for the little picaninnies. That's
>> for sure.

Other WOMEN enter and begin taking linen and
clothing, stuffing it into their own bosoms or waists.

> MAN
>> Let's burn it down!

> FIRST WOMAN
>> Wait! Let's go through the closets first.
>> There might be more clothing in there.

> WHITE MAN
>> You don't want hand-me-downs from no
>> blacks. You won't be able to get the stink
>> out of them.

The WOMEN ignore him and continue stuffing clothing into pillowcases.

> A THIRD WOMAN
> Look under the beds. There might be
> shoes. Oh, how I would love a pair of
> decent shoes for Katie. (Wistfully) Nine
> years old and she's never had a proper pair
> of girl's shoes.

> ANOTHER WOMAN
> (holding a coat)
> This is hemmed. I can let it out nice as
> you please.

CUT TO:
LONG SHOT: The front of the Colored Orphan Asylum. There are RIOTERS milling about the grounds. Some are throwing rocks through the windows. Through the broken glass we see the first flickering of flames.

CUT TO:
LONG SHOT of some wagons, plus a few coaches. The camera zooms in, and we see the CHILDREN from the Colored Orphan Asylum. They are singing and holding hands. The wagons are driven by blacks and whites.

INT. 7th DISTRICT POLICE STATION—SAME DAY

A number of BLACK PEOPLE are huddled together
on benches, obviously frightened. A man comforts
a woman who, in turn, has her arm around an older
woman, who rocks softly and hums. There are a number
of POLICEMEN trying to work around the people
seeking shelter.

> SERGEANT
> What's the situation in the park?

> OFFICER MCCLUSKER
> They're gathering their strength and
> drinking as much courage as they can
> find. We should close the bars.

> OFFICER BARNES
> The Dead Rabbits and the Bowery Boys
> are out with them, egging them on.

> OFFICER MCCLUSKER
> There's an old Colored granny over there I
> think I'll take around to my place. My missus
> will look after her. She's got no family.

> OFFICER BARNES
> We've got a few dollars in the precinct fund.
> Take what you need from there—anything
> to help these poor people. This is getting to
> be more and more of a cesspool. They killed

Colonel O'Brien of the 11th Volunteers—
did him in horrible, too—and all the
soldiers coming into the city are growing
uglier by the minute. There'll be more
widows than heroes before this thing is over.

OFFICER MCCLUSKER
And these poor devils don't know which
way to turn.

CUT TO:
A group of BLACKS huddled together in the station.

OFFICER MCCLUSKER
(cont'd)
They're chasing and beating every one
of them they find in the streets. Between
them torturing Negroes and stealing what
they can, they'll be up all the night.

OFFICER BARNES
We find the leaders and beat a tattoo on
their heads, and they'll soon come to their
senses. Give them enough headaches and
some time behind bars to let the whiskey
wear off enough, and the starch will leave
their backbones pretty quick. They'll see
they haven't gained anything for all their
strutting and boasting.

                    SERGEANT
It's not what a man has to gain that drives
him to the wildness; it's that he has
nothing to lose. This is going to be worse
before it smells of better. Believe me. A
messenger just came in from the First Ward
who said there's a crowd milling around
there, and there's more trouble a-brewing
at the armory. I don't much care if they
tackle the *Tribune*. They've got machine
guns in the offices to ward them off.

                OFFICER MCCLUSKER
In the building? They keep weapons in
the newspaper offices?

                 OFFICER BARNES
Nae, laddie, not on a normal day. But the
paper has hired some toughs and some
weapons. A bad business all around if you
ask me. This is all getting too ugly for words.

EXT. DOWNTOWN NEW YORK—SAME DAY

A CROWD has gathered on a street corner across
from the *Tribune* newspaper offices. We see JOHN
ANDREWS (41), a lawyer from Virginia and a Southern
sympathizer, stirring up the crowd. ANDREWS is a

smallish man with a neat beard. He is standing slightly behind LIAM, but close enough to whisper into LIAM's ear from time to time. ANDREWS rocks back and forth, sometimes even rising on his toes as he gets more excited.

> LIAM
>
> Lincoln is calling up the Irish to die for the darkies. It's not that I mind the dying if the cause is good. I'll take my chances along with the next man. I'll fight shoulder to shoulder to save my family and the scraps I've sweated for. At the Union . . .

> ANDREWS
>
> (whispers)
> Cooper Union.

> LIAM
>
> At Cooper Union, Lincoln said that he was fighting to preserve the Union, but we all know the real reason—to free the darkies so they can come and take what little chance we have to feed our own.

> CROWD
>
> You tell 'em! You tell 'em!
> (there is general cheering)

IRISH WOMAN
(to OLDER IRISH MAN on sidewalk)
>Well, they shouldn't be breaking things
up and hurting people no better off than
we are.

OLDER IRISH MAN
What?

IRISH WOMAN
>I'm saying that the Colored don't have
nothing either.

OLDER IRISH MAN
What?

IRISH WOMAN
>Oh, shut up!

LIAM
(looking around, building momentum)
>If the swells are so keen to be going to war,
let them stop their pretty speeches and put
down their silver snuff boxes and march on
down to the waterfront themselves. Sure
it's me and Mickey Mud and Paddy Stink
will follow right behind with our drums
beating and a screeching of the fifes.

ANDREWS
(whispers)
    Ten more years . . .

LIAM
    This war will go on for ten more years.
    Lincoln knows that. You know that. And
    it's all of us they'll be burying in shallow
    graves.

CROWD
    No! No!

CUT TO:
MEDIUM SHOT of LIAM and MAEVE, who has moved
by his side. He is becoming somewhat apprehensive,
while she stands with her hands on her hips. This is
clearly their moment.

CUT TO:
CLOSE-UP of ANDREWS. He is highly animated, and
we see his effect on the crowd as the camera moves slowly
around him.

ANDREWS
    There's more that think like us than
    think like them because there are more
    of us than there are of the dandies at the
    Tribune! What I'm saying is when they set

the type for the lists of dead soldiers, you
can be sure they don't find their own kin
there. You can believe that. We have to
organize, boys. Organize!

They're sitting behind those tall windows,
and they're asking themselves the same
questions we should be asking. They're
asking if the workers of New York City are
real men, or should we all be uptown on
the sheep meadow ready to be marched off
to whatever hell they've found for us? They
are asking the question and we have to give
them an answer!

CROWD

Men! We're men!
And women ready to fight by their side!

The CROWD grows more and more unruly as the
camera pulls back. The chanting becomes rhythmic,
almost heroic. The camera blurs slowly out of focus.

INT. THE PEACOCK INN—JULY 14, 1863—EARLY
MORNING

ELLEN is sitting in the semi-darkness of early morning.
JOHN enters the room, putting on his jacket. He stops
and looks at his wife.

JOHN

I'm off to see Dr. Smith. He has a cellar
door that needs fixing.

ELLEN

How much would you laugh if I told you
to be careful?

JOHN

I'm being careful. When fools don't care
who they kill, you have to watch yourself.
Some of the black men from the mill travel
together when they have to get somewhere.

ELLEN

Did you talk to Claire?

JOHN

She's keeping to herself.

ELLEN

Then we need to be where she is, John.
This hasn't been an easy time for her.

JOHN

(troubled)
Yeah, I know. I know.

ELLEN

She's not liking what she's been seeing,
that's for sure. And can we blame her?

JOHN

Who's liking what they see these days?
This is the second day and there's no
telling where it's going to end. They tore
up the Colored Orphan Asylum last night.

ELLEN

God! Where are the children? Priscilla?

JOHN

Safe for now. Some of them are in private
homes. Some are up in the Armory. Some
in police stations. They'll have to be
moved after a while, but they're safe for
now. There are still decent people in this
city. New York is still New York.

CLAIRE enters. She looks from her father to her
mother. ELLEN forces a smile.

ELLEN

Morning, love.

CLAIRE

Morning.

There is a pounding on the door.

JOHN

(calling out)
We're closed!

LIAM

(from outside)
It's me! Liam!

JOHN goes to open the door, and LIAM, MAEVE, and
ROSIE LYONS (14) enter. LIAM goes to a table and sits
heavily. MAEVE turns a chair and straddles it while
ROSIE sits across from them.

LIAM
I've been in the streets all night, Miss
Ellen. It's getting rough out there. People
being knocked around and worse. It's got
my head addled, it has. I need something
to eat.

ELLEN
We're closed until further notice, Liam.
You'll have to be getting your breakfast
elsewhere.

MAEVE
But he's hungry here, not elsewhere. And

we've got the money, haven't we?

                    JOHN
(sternly)
        She said we're closed, and she meant it.

                    ROSIE
        Is she the one you said was a blackie?

                    MAEVE
(indicating CLAIRE)
        She is. The one in green.

                    ROSIE
        Oh, she's a cutie.

                    JOHN
        I think it's time for you to leave, Liam.
        And take your friends with you.

                    LIAM
        Mr. Johnson, if this all doesn't come down
        on the right side, do you think I could be
        working steady at the Peacock?

                    JOHN
        What's the right side, Liam?

LIAM

It's hard knowing with all the shouting and
running through the streets, now isn't it?

CLAIRE

(Crosses to LIAM and takes his hand)
You're always welcome here, Liam. You
know that, don't you?

MAEVE

What is your name again?

CLAIRE

Liam must have told you that it's Claire.

MAEVE

Well, Miss Claire, don't be eyeing my
Liam. There's a lot more to me than you'd
be knowing, dearie.

CLAIRE

Eyeing Liam? I'm doing nothing of the sort!

ROSIE

I think she's in love, Maeve. She's blushing.

LIAM

Come on, I have to get home and get some

rest. Get me head together. Bye, Mrs.
Johnson. Claire.

MAEVE
(to CLAIRE)
You want to come with us? We'd love to
show you off to our friends.

JOHN
I said it's time for you to leave.

LIAM
We'll be seeing you later, then.

CLAIRE
Liam, be careful.

LIAM
That's for sure, Claire. Careful is me
middle name.

ROSIE
(as they leave)
If you ask me, she looks more German
than Irish.

LIAM, MAEVE, and ROSIE exit.

                    JOHN
Never mind that crowd. They don't even
know what they're doing. I'm headed
uptown. Lock the doors after me and stay
off the streets.

JOHN exits.
                    ELLEN
Are you all right, Claire?

                   CLAIRE
I hate people who don't even know what
they're doing.

                    ELLEN
Hate's a strong word for people you don't
know, Claire.

                   CLAIRE
That girl hates me because I'm black; I
can hate her because she's white.

                    ELLEN
Maybe she hates you because Liam has a
sparkle in his voice when he talks about
you. Now that would be a good reason not
to like you. Wouldn't it?

She crosses to CLAIRE and puts both arms around her.

CLAIRE starts to answer but instead begins to cry softly.

> CLAIRE
> Liam was just my friend a few days ago.
> We could laugh together, and I would kid
> him when he came to make deliveries.
> Now everything is upside down.

> ELLEN
> When things get back to normal around
> here we'll—

> CLAIRE
> They'll *never* be normal again.

Sobbing, she puts her head down as her whole body shakes.

> ELLEN
> When things come around—

The door to the Peacock opens.

> ELLEN
> (cont'd)
> We're closed! We're closed!

A thin white man, the poet WALT WHITMAN (44), enters, accompanied by FARLEY (11), a black boy, small for his age, whom he has hired to help him on his visit to New York. WHITMAN has been working as a nurse during the Civil War, but is far better known as a journalist and the poet who published *Leaves of Grass*. He looks much older than his age. He has a slight hesitant manner; he walks unevenly and leans on furniture as he passes.

                    ELLEN
(to WHITMAN)
        I told you we were closed!

                    WHITMAN
(seeing CLAIRE)
        Can I help? I have some experience as a nurse.

                    ELLEN
        No. And we're closed.

                    WHITMAN
        There's a covey of angry young men
        flapping and strutting their way down the
        street. I need to keep Farley here safe until
        they pass, and then we'll be on our way.

ELLEN looks at them cautiously and then goes and locks the door to the Peacock.

                    ELLEN
As soon as they pass . . .

                   WHITMAN
What happened?

                    ELLEN
A young man who worked for us has
joined the rioters. He brought some
friends by and they've upset my daughter.

                    CLAIRE
They don't like me because I'm black.

WHITMAN and FARLEY both turn and look at
CLAIRE, who lifts her chin proudly for a second but
then turns away.

                   WHITMAN
Well, I've seen them—swaggering through
the streets with crowd courage and
searching for themselves in the storm they
create with their shouts.

He settles at a table.

                    ELLEN
They're rioting in the streets. And stealing
what they can in the bargain.

CLAIRE

Last night they burned down the Colored
Orphanage.

WHITMAN

Yes, well, yes. I guess America has finally
shaken off the stupor of its promise and
its beauty and is asking itself questions it
should have answered seventy-five years ago.

ELLEN

Is it charms you're selling? Bibles? We
don't need charms and we have a Bible.

WHITMAN

I saw them lying on the battlefields and in
the hospitals in Washington. Sometimes
I would see them holding up little bits
of mirrors and staring at the strangers
looking out at them. In their hearts they're
asking what America means. They're
groping their wounds and their trauma and
searching for meaning to their lives before
those lives drip out onto the rich Southern
soil or in some obscure cow pasture.

CLAIRE

And who do you pretend to be?

WHITMAN
Pretend? Har! A good question. I am Walt
Whitman, newspaper reporter, sometimes
nurse, sometimes great poet, sometimes
an even greater drunk. And this is my
man Farley, who keeps my room clean up
at the Hotel Albert when I am out of town.
Farley is eleven years old and passes as a
fair philosopher. Am I right, Farley?

FARLEY
Yes, sir.

ELLEN
Well, if there's a thought in that crowd out
there it's running between their legs, not
dancing in their heads. That's for sure.
They're chasing black people in the streets.
They hanged a man on Baxter Street.

WHITMAN
Could I trouble you for a cup of tea?

ELLEN
(pours the tea)
Against my better judgment.

WHITMAN drinks from the cup and nods appreciatively.

WHITMAN

And if their lives have no meaning, they
pray that maybe the color of their skins
hold some vestige of a higher truth.

FARLEY

Did you see the way they was looking at
me? And I don't even know them, I don't.

CLAIRE

They're the ones who should have been
hanged.

ELLEN

My husband thinks they'll get tired of this
violence soon enough.

WHITMAN

It'll be done when America at last defines
itself, by what she sees in her collective
mirrors and not by what she sees in her
imagined world of snow white angels
floating among the clouds of our lofty
ideals. Until then, we'll all be in the streets
looking for where we belong.

ELLEN

And if that makes a bit of sense, I'm a
three-eyed bullfrog!

There's a pounding on the door and several shouts of rioters looking for drinks. The pounding continues for a long moment as the group inside is still, then stops as the rioters move on.

                    ELLEN
(cont'd)
     What do you know about violence? I can't
     see *you* as a soldier.

                    FARLEY
     He was in Washington.

                    WHITMAN
     And on the battlefields of Virginia. Treating
     the wounded of this terrible war. Holding
     the hands of better men than me and
     stronger boys as they waited to die. Keeping
     my sanity by not trying to make sense of it.

                    CLAIRE
     None of this is right. Why should anybody
     hate me because I'm black?

                    FARLEY
     You don't look black to me.

                    ELLEN
     I think the rowdies have passed. Perhaps
     you should go now.

WHITMAN

Farley, the lady wants us to leave because
you are black and therefore a danger and
I am a man with too many words for so
small an establishment. So we will go,
and try to keep our hind parts—yours
black and mine not capable of a decent
defense—off the winding streets of my
beloved city.

FARLEY

(to CLAIRE)

How you know you black? You don't look
black to me.

CLAIRE

I look black to me, Mr. Farley. I know what I
am and who I am and that's all that matters.

WHITMAN

And there you have the whole fish, Farley.
Head, gills, and tail. With that much
wisdom, we can upstream a-breeding go.

CLAIRE

Fish? Is that supposed to make sense? I
have no idea what that means, and I don't
want to know.

FARLEY

(as they head toward the door)
I don't think he knows, either, ma'am.

WHITMAN laughs as he and FARLEY exit.

ELLEN

(locking the front door of the Peacock)
Maybe your father is right. Maybe they'll
just grow tired of this running about and
go home.
(hesitates)
I'm thinking maybe we should take turns
looking out of the upstairs window in
case anyone comes looking for trouble.
We'd see them from a distance and be
ready for them. What do you think?
Though if only one or two came, we'd beat
whatever brains they had in their heads
till they weren't more than a pot of mushy
peas, wouldn't we?
(comes closer to her daughter)
Is that a bit of a smile on your lips? Is it
worth sharing?

CLAIRE

(in her best Irish brogue)
Ay, and it's happy I am to have a mum
such as yourself.

The two embrace briefly, and ELLEN pats CLAIRE on the shoulder.

                    ELLEN
        Ay, and it's happy I am to have a daughter
        sweet as you. I'll take a peek through the
        curtains.

ELLEN exits.

CLAIRE goes to the door and slides her fingers slowly along the black cast-iron bolt. She pushes the bolt open, then quickly closes it. We see a CLOSE-UP of her fingers nervously drumming against the heavy door.

                    CLAIRE
(voice-over)
        Maybe it's me who should be out there trying
        to find myself. Trying to discover who I am
        instead of hiding behind this door wondering
        who will find me and wondering what they
        will call me. I am afraid—not that they will
        hurt me but that they will discover who I
        am before I do. It would be better if they just
        hurt me, if they knocked me down in the
        street. Then I would just be me again, hurting
        and annoyed and even angry. But here,
        standing against this door, wondering what is
        happening on the other side . . . I am nobody.

We see her fingers again slide the lock open and shut.

> When they tell me that they are chasing
> black people in the street, I don't know
> what to feel. I am angry that anyone
> is being chased, but do I know what it
> means to be black? When that girl looked
> at me, it was with such contempt. A week
> ago she couldn't have hurt me. Now just
> the thought of her coming back fills me
> with terror. It's as if she has found who
> she is and can look right through me and
> know that I am lost.

Again she fingers the lock. The camera moves to the stairway.

> ELLEN

(calling from upstairs)
> Claire? Did you have anything for
> breakfast? Claire? Claire!

EXT. MADISON SQUARE PARK—SAME DAY

We see rows of tents, a few small fires, and groups of
SOLDIERS in small knots.

CUT TO:
Three privates, KELLY (25), PARKER (24), and

LANCASTER (17). KELLY and PARKER are both unshaven and have the look of men who have been in combat too long. LANCASTER looks (and is) too young to be in the army. His uniform hangs loosely on him. He stands while the other two soldiers sit. We see KELLY searching through his equipment bag, then walk away.

PARKER
He's got his mad on, but this has got to be better than facing Johnny Reb.

He is poking a small fire they have started, in which he has placed his canteen cup to make hot water for tea.

LANCASTER
I don't even know what this is about.

PARKER
About the draft. Something about the draft. These people don't want to enjoy the pleasures of marching in the sun.

LANCASTER
I heard the rebs had to kill a bunch of people to get them to report for duty.

PARKER
Captain said some of these people have

guns. Gotta be careful. A fool can kill you just as quick as a sniper. Gotta be careful.

LANCASTER
You had anything to eat? I'm starving.

PARKER
There's some eggs in that crate. They say don't suck them raw, but that's what I've been doing. You can boil them over the fire if you got a mind to. Don't boil them too long or they're get hard. I can't stand no hard eggs.

LANCASTER
Back home I used to suck them raw all the time. Go down to the henhouse and move an old fat biddy off her nest. I never figured out if they really cared or not. My ma didn't like it none, wanted me to sit around the table with my brother and daddy for breakfast. But my daddy never had nothing to say that wasn't grinding against the ear. Complainingest man I've ever known.

PARKER
That why you joined up? I thought you just liked the pretty brass buttons.

LANCASTER

Look at this one watching us. You figure
she's a spy or something?

The camera moves, and we see CLAIRE standing next
to a tree, about twenty feet from the soldiers.

PARKER

(calling to CLAIRE)
Come on over, darling. We won't bite you.

CUT TO:
CLOSE-UP of CLAIRE, who looks apprehensive, then
forces a smile. Return to MAIN SHOT.

PARKER

Lank here thinks you're a spy.

We see CLAIRE take a step back, then walk slowly
toward the soldiers.

PARKER

Morning!

CLAIRE

Morning.

PARKER

We're just here debating whether or not

Lank is going to die from eating raw eggs.
He says he won't, but I say he might. What
do you say?

CLAIRE looks from man to man but doesn't speak.

                    LANCASTER
I done ate raw eggs before, and there's
nothing to it.

                    CLAIRE
If you have a pan, I can cook them for you.

                    LANCASTER
We got a pan.

                    PARKER
Lank, you liable to come out this war a
man yet.
(taking loose tobacco and cigarette paper out of his
pocket)
        Got a woman cooking his breakfast! Miss,
        don't let his head get too close to your
        dress or it'll get all wet. He ain't got water
        on the brain; he's just a little wet behind
        the ears!

                    LANCASTER
Parker, you're a crazy man.

PARKER
(to himself as he heads off)
> Ain't but two months out of his diapers and
> he's got a woman cooking his breakfast!

CLAIRE and LANCASTER stand awkwardly, a few feet
apart. Then LANCASTER realizes what she is waiting
for and rummages through his bag. He produces a small
skillet and lays out the eggs, a piece of fatback, and a
heel of bread.

CLAIRE looks at the skillet closely, then takes
LANCASTER's canteen, pours water from it into the
pan, and wipes it out with the kerchief she takes from
her waist. She puts the skillet on the fire. After a few
seconds, the remaining water sizzles off.

CLAIRE
> You have a knife?

LANCASTER
(a bit cautiously)
> Yeah.

He gives her the knife and watches as she cuts off a
piece of the fatback and puts it in the pan.

LANCASTER
> You got a name?

CLAIRE

(more relaxed)
No, my parents were too poor to give me one.

LANCASTER

Get out of here!

CLAIRE

Claire.

LANCASTER

I'm Josh. Josh Lancaster. They call me
Lank, but you can call me Josh. Or Lank.
It don't matter.

We are watching CLAIRE cook the eggs and fatback.

CLAIRE

How old are you?

LANCASTER

Almost eighteen.

CLAIRE looks up at him quickly, realizing that he is
only a couple of years older than she is.

CLAIRE

How long have you been in the army?

LANCASTER
(trying to sound older)
    Long enough.

CLAIRE
Were you at Gettysburg? I read about the
battle there.

LANCASTER
You read? One day, when this war is all
over, I'm going back to school. Learn
reading and writing. Maybe geography.
Been a lot of places, so I got a leg up on
geography. I wasn't at Gettysburg. Met a
fellow who was there who read us a paper
on it. He said it wasn't nothing like it
happened, though.

CLAIRE
You have a plate?

LANCASTER
No, miss.

He takes the skillet from CLAIRE and attacks the breakfast.

CLAIRE
(stands as LANCASTER kneels)
    How was it different?

LANCASTER

(between mouthfuls)

He said it was mostly just sitting around
and waiting for something to happen.
Then there was a bunch of rebs charging
through a cornfield and yelling. That's
what them rebs do best. The rebs charged
and got beat back pretty good.

CLAIRE

Have you ever killed anybody?

LANCASTER

Don't know really. You shoot and you
hope for the best.

CLAIRE

Scared?

LANCASTER

Me? No, miss. Maybe . . . maybe a little.
Yes, miss, I was scared some. It wasn't the
dying that scared me. It was the wounded
laying out in the field calling out for their
mamas. That's a bad sound. That's a real
bad sound. Goes through you like a cold
wind. You can't relax after you hear a man
calling out, knowing he's . . . you know . . .
not going to make it.

CLAIRE

We had a man come into our hotel. My
family has a hotel. He said he was a nurse.
He said he had watched a lot of men die.

LANCASTER

I guess if your number is up. . . . How
good you read and write?

CLAIRE

Real good. *Very good.*

LANCASTER

(looks around)
I got a pencil and paper. You think you
can write a letter for me?

CLAIRE

Yeah.

The camera pulls back, and we see LANCASTER give
CLAIRE a pencil and paper. He has put the skillet
down and stands leaning on his rifle as he dictates the
letter to CLAIRE.

We hear LANCASTER's voice, young and a bit shaky, as
he dictates the letter.

LANCASTER
(voice-over)

Dear Mother,

I am doing well and hope this letter finds you
and the family safe and sound. Please tell
Uncle Phil that I saw a hog in Virginia that was
nearly a tall as his mule and was just as mean.
They don't have much for crops in Virginia
except tobacco and some measly wheat, which
I don't think they could sell on the fourth of
December, let alone the Fourth of July!

I am sorry to say that Michael Hansen,
who asked about our cousin Susan, was
wounded in the left shoulder. It didn't
look like much and he was in good spirits
but died anyway. I suspect his dying
surprised him as much as it surprised me.

I certainly miss Wisconsin and being home
and with you, Pa, Thomas, and Grandma
Ellie. I love you all very much and want you
to know that as a fact. This letter is being
written by a young woman from New York
City, and I will carry it with me for the rest
of the war and hope to bring it home to you.

Your loving son,
Joshua

                        CLAIRE
That's a nice letter.

                       LANCASTER
Thank you, miss.

                        CLAIRE
(looking for something to say)
        You . . . like being in the army?

                       LANCASTER
I did before I got into fighting. Then
there ain't nothing to like except feeling
yourself alive when it's done.

We see SOLDIERS forming up in the background.

                        CLAIRE
Why did you join?

                       LANCASTER
A man has to stand up for what he believes
in. I believe in God and my country and in
all people being free.

                        CLAIRE
Even black people?

LANCASTER

Don't make me no never mind what color
they are. I know I wouldn't want to be no
slave.

CLAIRE
(turns to face LANCASTER)
I'm black.

LANCASTER folds the letter and carefully puts it into his
vest. He looks up at CLAIRE, who is waiting for a reaction.

LANCASTER

Thank you for the eggs, miss. And for the
letter.

PARKER returns.

PARKER
Let's go, Lank. They're forming up.

We see LANCASTER and PARKER forming up with
their company.

LONG SHOT: The SOLDIERS begin to march, not
too smartly, out of Madison Square Park, headed
downtown. We see LANCASTER turn and look toward
where CLAIRE still stands. She waves. He touches his

chest where the letter is tucked.

CUT TO:
CLOSE-UP of CLAIRE watching the SOLDIERS. Then
we see her walk out of the park. She is lost in her thoughts
as she, too, heads downtown. Her step is light, almost
jaunty. She stops as she passes a store window to look at
herself and straighten her blouse before continuing.

EXT. A STREET NEAR THE PEACOCK INN—SAME DAY

A group of very YOUNG WHITE BOYS is taunting a
crippled BLACK MAN on one crutch as two STREET
TOUGHS watch. The BLACK MAN turns, stumbling,
as the TEENAGERS throw rocks at him.

CUT TO:
A plump WHITE WOMAN watching the scene, eyes
wide and her hand over her mouth as she wonders what
is going to happen.

CUT TO:
A window above the street. A SMALL BLACK BOY
looks down onto the street, his fingers anxiously
twisting the curtain, which half obscures his face.

CUT TO:
CLAIRE rounding the corner of a building. She sees the

taunting and stops in her tracks. For a moment she frowns.
Then she takes a deep breath and starts to move forward.

CUT TO:
From CLAIRE's POV: The BOYS are beating the MAN
up, kicking him when he falls and throwing rocks at
him.

                    CLAIRE
(softly)
          Oh, my God. Oh, my God.

Suddenly a hand appears over CLAIRE's eyes, and she
is jerked back violently.

                    CLAIRE
(in a panic)
          Oh! Oh!

CLAIRE is spun around and flattened against the
building. She is face-to-face with a smirking MAEVE.
BILLY EVANS stands next to her.

                    MAEVE
          Ho there, little blackie! Shall I go call the
          boys over so you can deliver your pretty
          speeches to them, eh? Shall I call them
          over, blackie?

CUT TO:

CLAIRE's terrified face. She starts to slide down the
building away from MAEVE.

> MAEVE
>
> Cat got your tongue, blackie? Is that it?
> Cat got your tongue now that you're away
> from your father?

MAEVE moves in front of CLAIRE and smacks her lightly.

> MAEVE
>
> (cont'd)
> Billy, why don't you give her a smack?

Full of bravado, BILLY puts the heel of his hand in
CLAIRE's face. Suddenly CLAIRE strikes out blindly,
hitting MAEVE, who stumbles backward into the
cobblestone street.

> MAEVE
>
> You little . . .

She touches her face as BILLY EVANS starts to kick at
CLAIRE. CLAIRE pushes him in the chest, and he falls
into MAEVE as she starts to get up.

CUT TO:

MEDIUM SHOT: We see CLAIRE running down the
street. MAEVE and BILLY follow for a few steps, then
stop. We see CLAIRE fall, get up, and continue running
toward the Peacock as the screen darkens.

INT. THE PEACOCK INN—SAME DAY

JOHN is near the door to the kitchen. ELLEN is across
from him, holding a towel in her hands.

                    JOHN
(shouting angrily)
        Where is she?

                    ELLEN
        I don't know! She was here in the dining
        room when I went upstairs, and when I
        called—

                    JOHN
        How long has she been out?

                    ELLEN
(sobbing)
        I don't know. Most of the morning.

                        JOHN
(sputtering)
        Why didn't you . . . ? Why didn't you . . . ?
        What did she say?

                        ELLEN
        She didn't say anything. I know she was
        upset and I tried to calm her down. I was
        trying to think of something for us to do
        together, to get her mind off of this, and—

There's a banging on the door, and JOHN runs quickly
to it and flings it open. ROBERT VAN VOORST
and GRIFFIN (15) enter. GRIFFIN is black, short
but sturdily built. His roundish face makes him look
somewhat younger than he is.

                        JOHN
        Have either of you seen Claire?

                        GRIFFIN
        No. Ain't she here?

                        JOHN
        Would I ask where she is if she was here?
        I'm asking—

                        ELLEN
        John!

JOHN

(calming himself)
>Okay. Okay. She went out this morning
>and—right now we don't know where she is.

GRIFFIN

>Some of the boys are thinking about
>getting together and facing these gangs,
>Mr. Johnson. I just come by to see if you
>want to join us.

ROBERT

>I've been thinking the same thing.

He produces a gun.

ELLEN

>Jesus, Mary, and Joseph! Are you out of
>your fool heads?

GRIFFIN

>Ma'am, we can't let these people just run
>around and beat us up and hang us. They just
>hanged another black man on the East Side.

JOHN

>Robert, put that damned thing away. They got
>the army and the police out there. We don't
>need to give them a reason to be shooting at us.

GRIFFIN

Mr. Johnson, I don't mean to be
disrespectful, but—

The door opens, and CLAIRE enters. The front of her
dress is covered with dirt, and her hair sticks to her face.

ELLEN

Claire!

JOHN

What happened? Are you okay?

CLAIRE

(tearfully)

Did you notice I wasn't human anymore?
That all I am is black? Did you know that?

JOHN

Baby, you're young. Right now all you need
to be is safe. Then we'll figure this all out.

ROBERT

Have you seen Priscilla?

CLAIRE

No, they've taken the children from the
orphanage and hidden them around the
city. She's probably with them.

JOHN
Are you hurt? Did they do anything to you?

CLAIRE
Pushed me down. Laughed at me. Nothing
that won't heal.

GRIFFIN
We need to get some revenge, Mr. Johnson.
We need to show them we can't be pushed
around so easy.

CLAIRE
Who's the "them" we going to go get, Griffin?
Who's the "them" we're going to get revenge
on? The same people we were laughing with
yesterday? How are they different today?

GRIFFIN
They weren't beating up black people
yesterday, Miss Claire. I think we should
go over to Jersey City and get some of
those black people just up from down
South. I hear there's a bunch of them just
waiting for some action.

ELLEN
(brings CLAIRE to a table and sits her down)
Griffin, if you could carry water the same

way you carry rumors, with not a vessel
to carry them in, you'd be a well. (to
CLAIRE) Do you need a doctor?

CLAIRE

No.

ROBERT

It's a dueling pistol, Mr. Johnson. English.

JOHN

Robert, shut up. You need to get your little
white butt home.

ROBERT

Sir, I'm looking for Priscilla.

JOHN

Boy, leave the gun here before you hurt
yourself with it. I'll get it back to your
father. You get out of here, walk down the
middle of the street, and go right home.
And don't leave your house until your
father gives you permission.

ELLEN

Until your *mother* gives you permission.
Now scoot!

ROBERT looks around the room. When his eyes meet
CLAIRE's, the two smile and CLAIRE throws him a kiss.

CLAIRE

When I see Priscilla, I'll tell her you were
looking for her.

ROBERT takes a deep breath, then leaves.

ELLEN

Claire, do you want tea?

CLAIRE

No. I want to sit here and be very angry. I
want to hate everybody and everything.

GRIFFIN

I know how she feels, Mr. Johnson. But if I
got to die, I'm dying like a man.

ELLEN

What we have to do—what we have to do
is to keep ourselves safe until this thing is
over. Then we'll sit down as a family—

CLAIRE

If it's my skin that makes me unsafe, can I
take it off and put it in a drawer until the

streets are calm again? If it's my skin that
puts me in the sights of murderers, can I
change it the way I would change my dress
or my apron? Where is this "safe" you're
talking about? And if I'm black and you're
white and that makes me a target, where is
this "family" you're talking about? Where
is it, Mum? Where is it?

There's a knock on the door.

JOHN
Griffin, sit over there, and keep your
mouth shut.

GRIFFIN sits down and puts the gun under the table.
JOHN opens the door and sees CHARLES HICKEY, a
tall, beefy patrolman.

HICKEY
Hey, John, glad to find you in. How you doing?

JOHN
Hickey, what you doing out here? I thought
you left the force and bought a warehouse?

HICKEY
(sits)
Bought it and working it part-time, John.

I figure to work it like this for a year and
then quit the force.

ELLEN
You being careful out there?

HICKEY
I'm trying to be, Mrs. Johnson. Between
the soldiers showing up and the gangs
running around I'm as nervous as a
country rat at a cat party. If John don't
want to come with me, I can understand it.

JOHN
Come for what?

HICKEY
I understand you know a lot of the
boatmen down at the piers.

JOHN
Yeah, I know most of them. The black
ones, anyway.

HICKEY
We want to get the children from the
orphanage out of the city. Take them out
to Blackwell's Island. We have a dozen
soldiers and half that many police officers

to guard them, but we need somebody that
the boatmen trust. We can't spare the men
to guard them night and day. We'll try to get
some of the kids out today and some later on.

ELLEN

John, you can't go out there—

JOHN

You're going to have to find someone else.
I got things I got to . . .
(looks toward CLAIRE)
You say we'll have an escort to the waterside?

HICKEY

A dozen good men. We just need someone
to deal with the boatmen.

JOHN

Okay, I'll go.

CUT TO:

CLOSE-UP of ELLEN's distraught face. We see her
mouth a vehement *No!* but no sound is heard. The
camera stays on ELLEN's face.

HICKEY

If we're going to get the children away, we
need to do it now.

ELLEN

No! Hickey, don't you see what's going on?

HICKEY

Yes, ma'am. I understand what's going on.
And I know who John is and what he stands
for. He doesn't have to go if he doesn't want
to, but I'm duty bound to ask him.

JOHN

Yeah, I got to go. This is a chance to get
the children to safety.
(glances toward Claire)
And we need to take that chance. I know
my way around this city.

ELLEN

(breathing deeply)
John . . .

JOHN

(picking up his vest)
Honey, I've got to go. Those children need to
be in a safe place. They'll attack the children
just to get the police away from the stores.
I'll be okay. Claire, you come with me.

CLAIRE

No, no, I'll be all right here.

JOHN

(sternly)

> You come with me, girl. Hickey, give us a
> minute.

HICKEY takes a look around and then steps outside.

CLAIRE

I'm not a child, Father. I'm not a child!
You need to help the children. I need to
stay here with Mother.

JOHN

(looks toward ELLEN)

> Girl, things might go well, and then again
> they might not. I might need all the help I
> can to get those children safe on board.

ELLEN

I'll go with you!

JOHN

No, you stay here. I'll be back as soon as I can.
Make sure the doors are locked, and don't
open them for anyone you don't know. Griffin,

you get your boys down to the waterfront in
case there's any trouble. Don't do nothing I
don't tell you to do. You got that?

GRIFFIN
I got it, Mr. Johnson.

JOHN, GRIFFIN, and CLAIRE exit.

We see ELLEN's hands tremble as she locks the door.
She leans against the door and the camera cuts to her
face. We see her lips moving and see her making the
sign of the cross as she prays.

EXT. ST. MARKS PLACE—SAME DAY

A CROWD of young men and women is standing on
the corner and taunting a group of SOLDIERS nearly
a block away. The SOLDIERS are setting up a Gatling
gun in the middle of the street. The camera switches
from one group to another. The SOLDIERS are lean,
battle-hardened men and seem particularly grim. The
camera moves in on three young people, KELLY, MARY
POOLE, and JOHNNY. KELLY is about nineteen, and
the other two fifteen.

KELLY
They're not facing a bunch of barefoot

rebels now, boys. We can show them
something to remember.

IAN

I got a bad feeling about this. This morning,
me mum was praying and her rosary beads
broke. It never happened before and she was
saying I should stay home.

MARY POOLE

The soldiers wouldn't shoot at us. Not
right at us, they wouldn't.

KELLY

Ian, you got to become a man sometime in
your life. You can't be a blinkin' boy forever.

JOHNNY

I'm not running, Kelly. All I'm saying is
that I got a bad feeling about this.

MARY POOLE

I think it's going to be all right, Ian. I do. I'm
scared, but I think it's going to be all right.

CUT TO:
The SOLDIERS, led by CAPTAIN ROBERTS. He is
unshaven, and there is a look of weariness about his eyes.

                    CAPTAIN ROBERTS
          We had two men hurt this morning.
          They're throwing rocks and bottles, and I
          hear that some muskets were taken from
          the armory. They're dancing in the streets
          as if this was some bloody game.

CUT TO:
LONG SHOT of the opposing groups. The CROWD
is beginning to pick up speed down the street. The
SOLDIERS almost nonchalantly raise their weapons.

                        CROWD
(voice-over)
          They're shooting to kill!
          Oh, sweet Jesus! My leg's on fire!
          Get down! Get down!

CUT TO:
PRIVATE LANCASTER as he reloads his rifle. He
glances down the street and sees the mangled bodies
from a distance. The camera blurs slightly, and it might
be that LANCASTER is crying. We see him touch
the front of his jacket where he is keeping the letter
CLAIRE wrote for him. We see him raise the rifle again.

Finally we hear the sound of the heavy breathing again,
and then that, too, subsides as we begin to FADE OUT.

CAPTAIN ROBERTS
Ready! Aim!

BLACK OUT as we hear another deafening volley.

INT. A DILAPIDATED TENEMENT BUILDING—SAME DAY

There is debris on the floor, and the curtains are torn.
In one corner there is a small potbellied stove on which
there sits a kettle. We see an OLD IRISH WOMAN
sitting near the stove with a cup of tea in her hands.
There is an OLD MAN standing near the window. His
hand shakes as he peers through the yellowed curtains.

OLD IRISH WOMAN
What's left after the young men fall?
When the young fall, there's no hope for
the old ones. There's faith and family and
not a whit more to fill the belly or turn
away the cold on a winter night. And
the saints, God bless them all, what are
they doing? Having tea with the swells
or a sour pint with the likes of Mickey
Mud? I don't know. For all my faith in the
Almighty, I don't know. What's left after
the young men fall?

The OLD MAN nods silently.

CUT TO:
LONG SHOT: There are a few people in the street
below. From the distance we can't tell whether they are
young or old, rioters or innocent victims. But we see
them move cautiously down the street, clearly afraid of
what is happening.

FADE OUT

FADE IN

EXT. THE WATERFRONT—SAME DAY

The CHILDREN from the Colored Orphan Asylum are
lined up, fairly orderly and holding hands. A YOUNG
BLACK MAN is leaning casually against a piling.
Under his jacket we see a glimpse of a club.

CUT TO:
A BLACK TEENAGER sitting on the edge of the pier, next
to a large cloth bag from which a stout stick protrudes.

CUT TO:
The face of a six-year-old BLACK GIRL. Her eyes are
wide, and there are tears on her face. We see that she is
holding someone's hand. As the camera moves back, we
see that it is PRISCILLA's.

CUT TO:

The first CHILDREN being passed into a small boat. They have pulled up along the pier next to the Hoboken ferry. The CHILDREN are being put quickly into the smaller boats. Two female ATTENDANTS from the home—one white, the other black—shelter the CHILDREN from the spray of water rising from the boats' engines.

CUT TO:

MEDIUM SHOT: JOHN stands face-to-face with CLAIRE. He seems huge as he faces his daughter.

> JOHN
>
> (pleading)
>> Claire, don't fight me on this. Please!
>> I need you to be safe. And yes, I know
>> you're not a child.

> CLAIRE
>> Then why are sending me off with the
>> children? Why?

> JOHN
>> It's for my sake. I need not to worry about you.

> POLICEMAN
>
> (not realizing that JOHN and CLAIRE are related)
>> You need help, miss?

                        CLAIRE
          No. No.

                        JOHN
          The very moment things have settled
          down, the very moment . . .

                        CLAIRE
          Father.

JOHN turns CLAIRE and pushes her to the boat where
the white woman ATTENDANT takes her.

                        JOHN
          (calling)
             I love you!

JOHN, on the verge of tears, looks over the water, then
a group of SOLDIERS passes in front of him. JOHN
moves down the pier, checking the other boats. Some
of the CHILDREN in the boats are anxious; some
are playing. JOHN nods to an older, white-haired
BOATMAN, then the boats begin to pull away. JOHN
watches the boats pulling away.

CUT TO:
MARGARET ADDAMS (32), a white matron at the
Colored Orphan Asylum. She is watching the last

of the CHILDREN board the boats. Next to her is PRISCILLA, and just beyond them, in the prow of a boat, we see CLAIRE.

> MARGARET ADDAMS
> Priscilla, get in. You'll be safe with us.

> PRISCILLA
> I'm not going. I have to see about my great-aunt. She's lame and she lives in Broadway Alley.

> MARGARET ADDAMS
> Well, you can't do that! You won't be safe on the streets, and we'll need you on the island to get things—Priscilla!

PRISCILLA turns on her heel and strides purposefully away.

CUT TO:
CLAIRE sees PRISCILLA on the shore. We see a CLOSE-UP of CLAIRE's face as her eyes widen. We see CLAIRE look around quickly, and then push her way through the crowd. We see her jump to the ladder, scrambling desperately not to fall into the water as the boat pulls away.

CUT TO:
JOHN, thinking that all of the children plus CLAIRE are on the boats, gives a hand signal.

CUT TO:

GRIFFIN, who stands and throws the bag he is carrying casually across his shoulder as he walks away from the waterfront.

CUT TO:

TWO BLACK TEENAGERS, who are leaning against a shed on the pier. They see GRIFFIN and follow him casually. We see that one of them is carrying an ax handle.

CUT TO:

JOHN as he peers anxiously at the boats. He is shielding his eyes from the late-afternoon sun, and his brow shows concern as he doesn't see CLAIRE.

CUT TO:

LONG SHOT of CLAIRE on the pier. She looks around and sees JOHN looking for her.

CUT TO:

JOHN. He is looking for CLAIRE and thinks he sees her, but his vision is blocked by the SOLDIERS headed away from the pier.

CUT TO:

CLAIRE, who ducks down and walks alongside the SOLDIERS until she is off the pier.

CUT TO:

PRISCILLA going west on Morris Street toward
Broadway. She keeps stopping and turning around as
people pass her. She is clearly afraid but moves on. We
see a figure coming up behind her. It is CLAIRE.

CUT TO:

CLOSE-UP: PRISCILLA sees CLAIRE and stops as her
friend catches up with her.

> PRISCILLA
>
> What are you doing here? I saw you on
> the boat.

> CLAIRE
>
> What are *you* doing here? Where are you
> going?

> PRISCILLA
>
> I'm going up to Broadway Alley to see
> about my great-aunt. She's so old and . . .
> fragile. I've been trying not to think about
> her. Is that terrible?

> CLAIRE
>
> There are a lot of things I've been trying not
> to think about, Priscilla. I'll go with you.

PRISCILLA
That's stupid. It's much too dangerous for you.

CLAIRE
Too dangerous for me? You're the one that's—

PRISCILLA
Black?

A beat as both girls assess their position.

CLAIRE
Priscilla, it's dangerous out here for both of us.

PRISCILLA
(turning away)
She's my aunt—I have to go. You go home.

CLAIRE
(hurt, on the verge of tears)
Then go!

PRISCILLA
All right, come along. But don't get in my way.

CUT TO:
MEDIUM SHOT: We see the two girls hurry along
Morris Street and then turn the corner at Broadway.

They are walking cautiously.

> CLAIRE
> I think things might be calming down a
> bit now that the soldiers are on the streets.

> PRISCILLA
> Claire!

We see a young BLACK MAN running out of Rector
Street. He is being chased by a group of white
RIOTERS. He is fairly young and runs well, with most
of the rocks and sticks thrown at him missing him.

PRISCILLA reaches out and stops CLAIRE.

> PRISCILLA
> Lord, when will it all end?

The camera pans down the street, and we see a knot of
SOLDIERS watching the whole affair. None of them moves.

Then we are back on PRISCILLA and CLAIRE and see
them turn and face each other as the RIOTERS, mostly
young men, pass them. The young men stop when they
see the SOLDIERS. One or two of them begin to throw
rocks at the SOLDIERS.

CUT TO:

A rock skips along the cobblestoned street and bounces
at the foot of a SOLDIER. Another rock hits the side of
a building and ricochets against a knapsack.

CUT TO:

MEDIUM SHOT: We see the SOLDIERS back away
a few feet. One rubs his palm on the stock of his
rifle. Another fixes his bayonet. Yet another begins
to unbutton his jacket. It is clear that they are ready
to respond. The RIOTERS sense this and move away
uptown, grumbling.

EXT. BROADWAY ALLEY—SAME DAY

Broadway Alley is a narrow, unpaved street, barely
twelve feet across, running between Twenty-sixth and
Twenty-seventh Streets just west of Third Avenue. On
the uptown end, there are poorly kept stables from
which there is a constant stench. There is smoke
coming from the windows of the west side of the alley.
A BLACK MAN is passing clothing through an open
window to a FRIEND. Both men are wary. The camera
moves cautiously down the alley.

                    RIOTER
(from off-camera)
          More darkies!

The MAN inside the window jumps out in a single move, and both MEN run toward the stables. They are chased by a group of RIOTERS. One of the BLACK MEN is hit in the back with a stick, but the assailant falls, tripping his laughing companions.

The attackers are bizarrely dressed, in regular clothing and some looted clothing, especially outlandish hats. They stop to see what the two black men were carrying out and pick up a Bible, which one shoves into his pants. The RIOTERS move out of the alley and saunter aimlessly down the street toward Third Avenue.

Two figures come into the alley from the Twenty-seventh Street side, and we recognize PRISCILLA and CLAIRE. As they come through the alley, a teenage BLACK GIRL climbs out of the same window that the BLACK MAN left moments before. The GIRL, startled by the presence of the two women, freezes.

> BLACK GIRL
> I don't have anything! Please don't hurt me!

> PRISCILLA
> We're not here to hurt you. Do you know
> my aunt? Her name is Esther.

CLAIRE

Mrs. Stephenson. She's an older woman. A friend. We wondered if she was all right.

BLACK GIRL

(obviously frightened)

She's all right. She's fine.

(points to a door opening)

She lives there, on the left side.

PRISCILLA and CLAIRE start toward the door as the BLACK GIRL leaves quickly.

PRISCILLA and CLAIRE enter an incredibly shabby room. CLAIRE instinctively covers her nose and mouth with her hand but still almost gags on the stench. There is a figure on the bed that we take to be PRISCILLA's great-aunt. PRISCILLA moves quickly to the bed and starts to speak as she touches the old woman's shoulder.

PRISCILLA

Aunt Esther! It's me, Priscilla. We'll take you to a safe . . . place. . . .

CLOSE-UP to MEDIUM SHOT to CLOSE-UP from behind as PRISCILLA realizes that the old woman is dead. PRISCILLA shrinks away, her hands over her face.

CUT TO:

MEDIUM SHOT: CLAIRE goes to PRISCILLA and pulls her away.

> CLAIRE
> Are you sure?

> PRISCILLA
> Oooh. Claire, she's cold. Oh, my God.

> CLAIRE
> Let's . . . Priscilla, let's leave now.

As PRISCILLA and CLAIRE are leaving the apartment, CLAIRE turns and takes one more look around at the condition of the room, knowing that it was never in much better condition. She is still covering her nose and mouth with her hand as they move out into the alley.

EXT. BROADWAY—SAME DAY

CLAIRE and PRISCILLA are walking downtown rapidly toward the camera. As they pass Nineteenth Street, they see a CROWD of young whites milling about. They stop to survey the situation.

CUT TO:

A BLACK WOMAN and her CHILD come down the

street, followed by some very small white children.
The WOMAN, holding the CHILD by the hand, turns
back and starts in the other direction but is cut off. A
WHITE WOMAN pushes her down roughly.

CUT TO:
CLOSE-UP face of the BLACK CHILD. He is terrified.

VOICE-OVER: What are you doing? Have you lost
your minds?

CUT TO:
MEDIUM SHOT of CAITLIN DONAHUE, 16, 5'2"
with red hair and green eyes. We see her throw both
arms around the black child.

> CAITLIN DONAHUE
> Have you lost your minds for sure? Does
> it make you proud to be throwing your
> weight at a little child? Do you have no
> shame in you?

MEDIUM SHOT: We see the other women look away.
Then one helps the BLACK WOMAN up.

CUT TO:
CAITLIN DONAHUE puts the child's hand in that of
the mother.

CAITLIN DONAHUE
(to the BLACK WOMAN)
They're not really Irish, don't be
minding them.

The camera seems to dart around as small groups of
whites are moving onto Broadway, where CLAIRE and
PRISCILLA have stopped.

We hear he sound of a heartbeat as CLAIRE becomes
more and more anxious about their position.

CLAIRE
Let's get off Broadway. We'll go west.

A CROWD is gathering on one side of Broadway.

PRISCILLA and CLAIRE are walking on the opposite side
of the street from the CROWD, arm in arm, heads down.

We see the sidewalk from CLAIRE's POV, and then the
legs of a person in their way as we hear the impact of
the light collision.

CLAIRE
Oh, I'm sorry!

The camera pans up on MAEVE's face.

> MAEVE

Oh, and what do we have here? The
lovelies out and about the streets of New
York! Out seeing the sights, are you?

> PRISCILLA

We're on our way home. You're in our way,
so if you would just step aside . . .

MAEVE pushes up on PRISCILLA.

PRISCILLA freezes for a moment and then attempts to
step around MAEVE, who pushes her against the steps
of a brownstone. MAEVE steps back and calls to her
friends in the crowd.

> MAEVE

Hey, look what we've got over here!

LIAM calls over.

> LIAM

They've broken into Goodman's! Let's get
over there!

> MAEVE

(to CLAIRE)
I didn't think you'd have the nerve to

show your face, dearie. You having a good
time, are you?

LIAM

Maeve, it's Goodman's. Let's go.

He starts to back away, anxious to get on with the looting.

MAEVE

Liam, this is the darky lover who said I
wasn't good enough to work in her place.

LIAM looks and recognizes PRISCILLA and CLAIRE

LIAM

(takes CLAIRE's face in his hands)
Claire, you can't be on the street. It's not
safe out here for anybody. It's not, I'm
telling you. Go home and stay there till
this is over.

MAEVE

(stunned)
Are you sweet on her? Are you sweet on
her? Liam, I'm your . . . Liam, she's . . . black.

Liam starts off, hoping Maeve will follow.

MAEVE watches him go and then turns back to CLAIRE.

MAEVE
(to CLAIRE, as CLAIRE and PRISCILLA walk
quickly away)
    You're black!

CUT TO:
MAEVE watches CLAIRE go off, her face confused and
angry, and then she runs off after LIAM.

CUT TO:
MEDIUM SHOT: PRISCILLA and CLAIRE run down
the street as the RIOTERS are headed the other way,
toward Goodman's.

We hear the sound of heavy breathing as we follow
PRISCILLA and CLAIRE down a city block and around
a corner. Finally PRISCILLA stumbles against the fence
of a small churchyard.

PRISCILLA
(panting)
    They won't be happy until they kill us all.

CLAIRE
(mouth open, partially bent over)
    God, I can't believe that only a week ago I
    was just Claire. Now what am I?

                    PRISCILLA
      Do you think they'll come to the Peacock
      after us?

                     CLAIRE
      I don't know. I don't know.

                    PRISCILLA
      Are you all right?

                     CLAIRE
      No.

              A BLACK MALE VOICE
(from off-camera)
      If you're scared, children, you're welcome
      here.

PRISCILLA and CLAIRE are both startled. They look
up to see a black man in a preacher's garb.

                    REVEREND
      I'm Reverend Curry. Our church is always
      open for anyone who needs refuge.

CUT TO:
The front of a black Baptist church. An OLDER MAN
stands in the doorway at the top of some steps.

PRISCILLA and CLAIRE hesitate for a moment, then
quickly go to the church and up the steps. Several
YOUNGER MEN are standing near the door. One of
them has a rifle, and another has a pistol.

> REVEREND CURRY
> (nods toward the armed men)
> (to PRISCILLA and CLAIRE as he enters the church
> with them)
>> "He that hath no sword, let him sell his
>> garment, and buy one." Now may not be
>> the time to turn the other cheek.

The camera pans the interior of the church. It is dark
except for the late-afternoon light coming through the
stained-glass windows and a few candles. There are
shadowy figures, and we see BLACK PEOPLE in small
groups. Some are praying.

CUT TO:
CLOSE-UP: CLAIRE is wide-eyed as she looks around
the church. We hear a BLACK WOMAN singing; she is
joined in a rich but subdued harmony of earnest voices.

> SINGERS
> (from off-camera)
>> You hear the lambs a-crying,
>> Hear the lambs a-crying,

Hear the lambs a-crying,
Oh, shepherd, feed-a my sheep.

CUT TO:
CLOSE-UP: A BLACK WOMAN, one of the singers,
heavy in her shoulders and bosom, caught up in the
passion of the song, and of the moment.

                    SINGERS
(cont'd)
          I don't know what you stay here for,
          Don't know what you stay here for,
          Don't know what you stay here for,
          Oh, shepherd, feed-a my sheep.

          Our Savior spoke these words so sweet:
          "Oh, shepherd, feed-a my sheep."
          Said, "Peter, if you love me, feed my
          sheep."
          Oh, shepherd, feed-a my sheep.

CUT TO:
MEDIUM SHOT: We see the involvement of the entire
church, the light subdued, candles away from the
windows, sweat gleaming from black faces.

We hear an angry crowd outside, shouts and curses.
But inside, the quiet singing continues. A YOUNG

BLACK BOY reaches out and takes CLAIRE's hand.
He smiles shyly at her.

CUT TO:
CLOSE-UP of CLAIRE's face as she smiles back, but
her eyes are teary as she realizes that this is a side of
black life she knows nothing about.

                    SINGERS
(cont'd)
          Oh, Lord, I love Thee, Thou dost know;
          Oh, shepherd, feed-a my sheep.
          Oh, give me the grace to love Thee more;
          Oh, shepherd, feed-a my sheep.

CUT TO:
We see CLAIRE AND PRISCILLA sitting in the pews
with the black parishioners.

CUT TO:
CLOSE-UP of a clock on a shelf. It is four thirty.

CUT TO:
The outside of the church. It is beginning to rain. A
horse-drawn carriage approaches. A SERVANT
WOMAN appears at the gate of a house on the street; she
opens the gate and the carriage goes in. The DRIVER
gets out, looks around cautiously, and locks and padlocks

the gate. He throws a blanket over the horse and quickly
goes into the house.

CUT TO:
INT. of church. CLOSE-UP of clock. It is five thirty.

CUT TO:
PRISCILLA, CLAIRE, and REVEREND CURRY at the
front of the church.

>REVEREND CURRY
>Things look a little quieter now. The rain
>will help. But you are welcome to spend
>the night here.

>PRISCILLA
>Thank you. Thank you so much. But we'd
>better be getting along now.

>REVEREND CURRY
>Then feel free to come any Sunday.

>CLAIRE
>(quietly, almost to herself)
>I will, I will.

EXT. MERCER STREET—SAME DAY

We are looking from south to north up Mercer Street
at a group of weary SOLDIERS. Two of them stand in
front of a boarded-up window. Above the boards we see
the sign GOODMAN'S FINE GOODS.

FIRST SOLDIER
You know, I got a daughter almost six
months old I haven't seen. I'd love to see her
before I die. I thought I always wanted a boy
child, a son. When April told me the baby
was a girl, I was disappointed at first. Then
I started thinking about the little girl, and
I found myself crying because she was so
beautiful. Ain't that something? She being
so beautiful and all and me never having
laid eyes on her? Ain't that something?

SECOND SOLDIER
That's something, all right.

FIRST SOLDIER
You hear what Beck said the other day?
He said he clean forgot what this war was
about. Except for the killing, of course.

SECOND SOLDIER
(eyeing rioters down the street)
They forming up down there?

FIRST SOLDIER

I guess. They ain't seen enough dying to
back off from it. They will by and by. They
will by and by.

OFFICER

Lock and load!

CUT TO:

A group of Irish YOUNGSTERS. Some are teenagers,
but they are mostly boys, with a few girls among them.
They are boisterous, excited, young. They mock the
SOLDIERS and begin to throw small rocks. We see one
of the rocks bounce along the street and land at the foot
of a SOLDIER. The camera pans up on the face of the
SOLDIER. We recognize him as JOSHUA LANCASTER.

CUT TO:

CLOSE-UP: The face of a YOUNG MAN among the
rioters. He is anxious.

CUT TO:

CLOSE-UP: Another face. This one is even younger.

CUT TO:

CLOSE-UP: Another face. We recognize BILLY EVANS.

CUT TO:

MEDIUM SHOT: We see the RIOTERS as a group.
They are looking down the street at the SOLDIERS,
wondering what is going to happen. We see MAEVE
join the crowd. She is looking around for LIAM.

                    YOUNG MAN
(to someone off-camera)
          Hey, you. Take some boys and get in front of
          the soldiers so they don't see what's going on.

                    LIAM
(as he is joined by MAEVE)
          Get in front of the soldiers yourself!

                    YOUNG MAN
          Go on! We'll see that you're taken care of.
          Go on!

CUT TO:

A MAN whom LIAM knows gives him the thumbs-up sign.

CUT TO:

LIAM takes a hesitant half-step forward, then inhales
deeply. WE HEAR the sound of a low note from a cello
that begins to rise in volume.

CUT TO:
The older YOUNGSTERS push the CHILDREN
forward. The SOLDIERS stand and form a loose line.

STREET TOUGH
They won't shoot. What do they care about
Goodman's?

CUT TO:
CLOSE-UP: JOSH LANCASTER, biting his lip anxiously.
The camera moves from face to face, and we see that the
RIOTERS are clearly apprehensive about the SOLDIERS.

CUT TO:
TOMMY ENRIGHT and DENNIS RILEY among the
crowd.

TOMMY ENRIGHT
(getting up his nerve)
We get in and we get out quick! Bam!
Bam! Bam! Nothing to it.

DENNIS RILEY
You sure we can trust the kid? If he takes the
goods down to bleedin' Mulberry Street . . .

TOMMY ENRIGHT
(glancing toward the soldiers)

You losing your backbone? You going
yellow?

DENNIS RILEY

(nervously)
No. No. I don't think they'll open up on us.

TOMMY ENRIGHT
I ain't scared none.

CUT TO:
LONG SHOT of the opposing groups. The RIOTERS
are beginning to start toward the SOLDIERS. The
SOLDIERS almost nonchalantly raise their weapons.
Among the RIOTERS, we recognize the signature
ribbons of the Dead Rabbits. They stop in front of
Goodman's but point toward the SOLDIERS.

Suddenly a brick is produced and thrown through
the window of the store. We hear shattering glass,
punctuated by the shouts of bravado from the onrushing
RIOTERS as the camera assumes their POV. Then there
is the deafening noise of a volley from the SOLDIERS.

CUT TO:
A YOUNG MAN has fallen. He looks down at his
bloody chest and, childishly, tries to wipe away the hurt.
There is a spreading stain on his chest and a look of

incredulity on his face as he realizes he is dying.

CUT TO:
The distraught face of an OLD WOMAN. She shakes
her head and clutches her rosary beads tightly.

> TOMMY ENRIGHT
> Hold it! Move to the sidewalks! Look out
> for the wounded!

We hear a second deafening volley from the army.

More of the RIOTERS fall, including at least one woman.
People are running, bumping into each other. A woman
reaches down for the outstretched arm of a child.

We hear very heavy breathing and the sound of a person
in pain. The sound is almost a whimper that grows in
volume and then fades. Finally we hear the sound of the
heavy breathing again, and then that, too, subsides.

CUT TO:
CLOSE-UP of MAEVE kneeling on the ground next to
the lying figure of LIAM.

> MAEVE
> (screaming)
> Liam! Liam!

LIAM
(his mouth open, frantically sucking in air)
Oh! Oh!

MAEVE
Oh, please! Speak to me, Liam. Speak to me!

The camera looks over MAEVE's shoulder to LIAM. He
is searching MAEVE's face, but he is holding his chest.
He moves his hand away, and we see an angry red
splotch on his shirt and vest.

LIAM
Am I all right, love?

MAEVE
(looking at her blood-splattered hands)
Yes. Yes. You're going to be just fine,
darling. Just fine.

CUT TO:
MEDIUM SHOT from a rooftop: Several people lay
wounded in the streets. Those who are not wounded are
trying to care for them. We hear the sound of an Irish folk
tune. It is far too gay for the grim scene we are visiting.

CUT TO:
CLOSE-UP of an OLD MAN's face as he looks at the

wounded. He is shocked and somewhat dazed.

CUT TO:
CLOSE-UP of a SOLDIER's face. The camera moves in, and we see that the SOLDIER is younger than we first thought. His eyes are wide, his breathing shallow. He has not expected to be shooting civilians.

FADE TO BLACK.
INT. THE PEACOCK INN—SAME EVENING

CLAIRE and PRISCILLA are sitting at a table, both clearly tired and distressed. JOHN is standing, and ELLEN sits and rocks on another chair.

JOHN
Where were you? I was looking . . . I put you on the boat myself!

CLAIRE
I got off the boat. I am not a child.

JOHN
(sputtering somewhat)
You disobeyed me! I am your father!

ELLEN
Don't yell at her! I'm here! You're here! We're a family!

JOHN

Ellen, it's my place to see to the safety of
my family.

CLAIRE

Aren't we all just learning our places here?
Aren't we finding them like that poet said?
They're finding them in the fires we're
setting, and we're finding them, too. I didn't
choose to be black.

ELLEN

Claire!

CLAIRE

I didn't! I just wanted to be a human being. I
just wanted to be whoever I saw in the mirror,
without a race or a place in life. What is so
wrong with that? What is so *wrong* with it?

JOHN

Claire, there's nothing wrong with you
being you. I love who you are and will until
I die. But first, first we need to get through
these hard days.

CLAIRE

I know. I know. But what will we be when
we come out of them?

ELLEN

Priscilla, are you all right, child?

PRISCILLA

We went to my aunt's house. She's dead. I
don't know what happened.

ELLEN

Oh, my God! I'm so sorry.

JOHN

How are you, Priscilla?

PRISCILLA

As well as I can be, I guess.

JOHN

Your father sent a message by a salesman
coming into New York. He asks me to
let you stay with us if I can find you. Of
course you can stay here.

ELLEN

Things will get better. They're saying that
the streets are calming down now.

JOHN

After three days, maybe they've done all
the damage they can.

CLAIRE

I'm sorry you were worried. But I couldn't
just run away with the little children. I
have to find myself. Face up to who I am.

ELLEN

And who can that be, Claire? And who is
doing the telling? Is it you or is it those
people screaming down the streets?

CLAIRE

It's me, Mum. It's me looking at myself
and finding a black woman where there
was only a girl before.

ELLEN
(goes to CLAIRE)
And who am I, darling? Where have you
found me?

CLAIRE

You're still my own sweet mum. I just have
more parts to fit in than I thought.
(the two embrace)

ELLEN

More parts than I ever thought.

CLAIRE

Maybe, when this is all over, when the
streets are quiet again, we'll be able to
sit down and sort it all out. Maybe one
day we can even forget about the ugliness
and not worry about what color we are.
We can just be the Johnson family, proud
owners of the Peacock, the best place in
New York City. And anyone who walks
through our front door can just be a
human being. Just a human being.

ELLEN

And we'll steal Priscilla from her parents
to supervise the cleaning staff. Which will
probably mean me and Claire.

CLAIRE

(as we slowly fade out)
It'll be a grand place. And I can go back to
being Claire again. Is that possible? That I
can just be myself again?

FADE OUT

INT. THE PEACOCK INN—LATE THAT NIGHT

We open on a darkened screen with some light bleeding

in from the left. The camera moves slowly to the left,
and we see a small votive candle on a corner table.

We hear the sounds of heavy breathing as if someone is
carrying a heavy burden. Along with the burden there
are sounds of distress as well in the breathing pattern.

We see, dimly, a mouse moving along the floor. It is
tentative, stopping now and again, lifting its little snout
into the air as if finding its way by scent. The camera
moves with the mouse slowly, then quickly as it climbs
the leg of a table.

We see the crouching figure of a cat. It moves, its
body low to the ground, almost imperceptible in the
darkened Peacock.

We hear, again, the sound of labored breathing, then
banging against the door.

We see the mouse, alert, scurrying down from the table.
We see the cat freeze, one paw in the air, then move
silently into the shadows.

We hear more banging against the door, this time more
urgent.

CUT TO:

CLAIRE's bedroom. We see fingers over a dampened oil lamp. The fingers turn up the lamp, and we see CLAIRE's face, half lit by the lamp. Her eyes are wide. Dressed in her nightclothes, she moves quickly from the bed and to the door. At the door, she stops and turns, and we see PRISCILLA still lying on the bed.

CLAIRE enters her parents' bedroom. JOHN is already up and is pulling up his trousers.

                    JOHN
        Late-night drunks. I'll tell them we're closed.

                    CLAIRE
        It could be black people, looking for
        shelter.

                    JOHN
        I'll them we're closed, honey. The rioting
        has died down for now. They'll be safe
        until morning.

JOHN and CLAIRE go down the stairs to the main floor of the Peacock.

                    ELLEN
        (from the bedroom)
            What are you doing?

JOHN

(over his shoulder)
> Go back to bed.

ELLEN

(pulling her robe closed as she joins JOHN and
CLAIRE on the stairs)
> Oh, yes, of course.

JOHN, CLAIRE, and then ELLEN reach the first floor.
They all look toward the front door, and again we hear
the banging. JOHN crosses to the window and looks out.
The camera looks out with him, but we can't see anything
significant. JOHN picks up a poker and hefts it to feel its
weight. CLAIRE looks around and picks up a candle.

JOHN

(at the door)
> The Peacock is closed. Go home.

MAEVE

(from outside)
> It's Maeve. And Liam. Oh, he's hurt so
> bad. We need help.

JOHN

> I'm sorry, but . . .

MAEVE

Please.

ELLEN goes to the door. She starts to unlatch it when
JOHN puts a hand on her shoulder and shakes his head no.

MAEVE

Please, he just needs a little water.

ELLEN turns to JOHN, her eyes pleading. JOHN steps
back, his muscles taut in case it's a trick. ELLEN lifts the
latch and unlocks the door. MAEVE and JOSEPH, a gang
member, half drag, half carry LIAM into the Peacock.

MAEVE

Oh, thank God. The soldiers are rounding
everybody up, even the wounded ones.
People are dying in the streets, and in the
houses, and everywhere you have a mind
to look. Oh, my sweet Jesus. Did you say
you worked for a doctor? Do you think you
could get him to come and look at my Liam?

They bring LIAM, who looks terribly wounded, into the
Peacock and lay him down on a table. The camera pans
his body, and we see an incredibly large bloodstain on
his shirt which also covers the upper half of his pants.
We go to his face for an instant and quickly away, as if
even the camera cannot stand to see what it must see.

Then the camera moves back to LIAM's face, and we
see a young man minutes from the dying.

                    JOSEPH
(nervously)
        I'll be on me way.

                    MAEVE
(to JOSEPH)
        Thank you.
(then to JOHN as JOSEPH leaves)
        Do you think the doctor will come?

                    JOHN
        Let me get his shirt open.

                    MAEVE
        He's bleeding so . . .

CUT TO:
CLOSE-UP of ELLEN's face as she stares wide-eyed
past JOHN.

                    ELLEN
He needs a doctor.

CUT TO:
MEDIUM SHOT: LIAM is on table, CLAIRE is getting
water.

JOHN

No doctor will come out in this madness.

CLAIRE

He'll die without a doctor.

MAEVE

He's really an all-right sort. He is. Really.
And strong. If we can bring him around,
he's strong enough to pull through. I
know he's strong enough to pull through!

ELLEN

John? John?

JOHN

I'll go look for a doctor. Maybe Dr. Smith,
if they haven't hanged him or beaten him
to death.

MAEVE

(to CLAIRE)
Do you think he'll be all right?

CLAIRE

Yes, I'm sure.

MAEVE watches as JOHN goes to the door. It has started to rain.

                    MAEVE
(looking anxiously about)
        We weren't meaning what we said before.
        About coloreds and that sort of thing. It
        was just . . . a bit of a lark.
(voice trailing as she realizes the position she is in)
        Not a very good lark. We didn't mean any
        harm.
(begins to pray for LIAM)
        Oh, God, he's not a bad sort. He's not a
        bad sort. He likes people. Oh, won't you
        people say something. Please, he's not a
        bad sort. Really.

CLAIRE puts her hand on MAEVE's and bows her head.

                    MAEVE
(continues praying)
        Oh, God, please don't let him go.
        Everything he's ever done wrong, he's
        sorry for, and everything he's done right,
        he meant to do well.

We hear MAEVE still praying for LIAM.

We see LIAM absolutely still.

We see LIAM move slightly, make a very feeble sign
of the cross, then lift one arm as if he is reaching for
something high above him. We see the arm come down
slowly. We see LIAM's face blanch and then his head
turn slowly to one side.

                    MAEVE
          Liam? Oh, Liam.

We hear the sound of music rising in pitch until it is
indistinguishable from the high wailing of a scream.

DISSOLVE

EXT. WASHINGTON SQUARE—JULY 15, 1863—
MORNING

MEDIUM SHOT: A NEWSBOY is selling papers. Two
GENTLEMEN take papers, and one tosses a coin
toward the boy.

                 FIRST GENTLEMAN
          Well, it's over at last. None the worse for
          the city, if you ask me. Gives us an air of
          neutrality.

SECOND GENTLEMAN
I heard the federal government is going to
pay for all the damages.

FIRST GENTLEMAN
I wasn't damaged. And with the
government handing out money, there
won't be too many hurting.

EXT. A CATHOLIC CHURCH—SAME DAY

A solemn procession of MOURNERS leaves the church.
They carry two caskets. The first is full size, the second,
in the arms of a beefy IRISHMAN, much smaller.

EXT. A CEMETERY—SAME DAY

Small GROUPS OF PEOPLE are gathered around
several grave sites.

CUT TO:
The craggy face of a black UNDERTAKER wearing a
top hat. He looks straight ahead as we hear the voice of
a black MINISTER.

MINISTER
(voice-over)
For I have laid me down on holy ground,

and in the darkest hour I have lifted mine
eyes unto the hills and there I have seen
salvation. . . .

EXT. A BLACK BAPTIST CHURCH—SAME DAY

A sad CONGREGATION files out of the church,
carrying a casket.

CUT TO:
Two small BOYS, one white and one black, standing on
a corner watching the funeral processions.

EXT. A TENEMENT BUILDING—SAME DAY

A group of roughly dressed YOUNG WHITE MEN is
carrying a casket down a flight of wooden steps. A
PRIEST walks in front and past a group of sad-faced
WOMEN. One of them turns abruptly away.

CUT TO:
CLOSE-UP of her profile; we recognize MAEVE.

FADE OUT

FADE IN

INT. THE PEACOCK INN—SAME DAY

JOHN, ELLEN, and CLAIRE are gathered around a
table. There is bowl of fruit on the table illuminated
by the slanting rays of the afternoon sun. JOHN is
cleaning the bottom of a copper pot. ELLEN and
CLAIRE sit as if they are tired.

                    CLAIRE
        At least things are calmer now.

                    JOHN
        They still haven't brought the children
        back from Blackwell's Island.

                    CLAIRE
        Where are they going to bring them with
        the orphanage burned down?

                    JOHN
        They took some to Weeksville, in
        Brooklyn. Brooklyn's a good city.

                    ELLEN
        The police are rounding up the last of the
        hooligans. Did you hear—?
(nervously as she wonders how all that has happened
will affect her family)
        Have you eaten anything?

JOHN

I'm not hungry.

ELLEN

(a beat)

Did you hear they were going house to
house on Worth Street looking for stolen
goods? And once the police get the goods,
they'll just end up in a different house. I
don't trust the police any more than I did
the toughs in the street. But they'll not
be rioting in the streets of New York for
a while. Leastways those who know the
difference between a duck and a spade.

JOHN

And life goes on.

CLAIRE

Priscilla was mixed about leaving today.
She was sad going to Connecticut, even
for the while, but relieved not to be afraid
of walking down a street. It's sad to think
of how we were just dancing down these
same streets on the Fourth of July.

Do you think that you can have another talk

with Mr. Valentine, now that things are quiet?

                    JOHN
He was clear when he spoke to me the
first time, and clearer yesterday when I
asked him if I could add more fish to the
dinner menu. He looked me in the eye. . . .
He looked me in the eye and said that I
would have to consult the new owners.

I asked him if he didn't mean the new
white owners, even though they made an
offer that was less than ours? He said he
had an obligation to the community. Then
he looked away. Just looked away.

SLOW DISSOLVE

INT. NASSAU HALL LIBRARY, PRINCETON

ROBERT VAN VORST sits at a desk, talking to two
older STUDENTS who stand near him. After a brief
conversation, the two leave and ROBERT picks up his
pen and begins writing.

                    ROBERT
(voice-over)
        Dear Claire,

Well, I'm firmly ensconced (a new word)
at Princeton now. I haven't made any real
friends, and it's quite strange to be only in
the company of boys all the time. We are
not supposed to talk about the war, but
that is really all that we talk about when
someone is not arguing about religion,
which is also a less than temperate topic
here. Some of the Southern boys have
actually brought their Negroes with them
as servants. Living in New Jersey, they
have to be free, of course, but I sense a
kind of understanding that makes them
somewhat less than completely free.

Oh, how I miss our running down to the
docks and watching the ships come in.
We study geography and learn of many of
the places from where the ships sail, but I
believe it more fun to imagine the places
than to be burdened with actual knowledge.

I also miss your laughing. It always seemed
that you laughed a lot, and that made me
feel good even on the gloomiest of days.

Father writes me dutifully once every
two weeks, giving me parental advice.

Sometimes the other boys compare their
letters from home, and it is amazing how
similar they all are. He tells me that the
best guess is that the South will lose the
war and that will make an end to slavery.
I hope that is true because the words
of the founding fathers—did you know
they sometimes met at Princeton?—did
promote freedom for all peoples.

I wrote to Priscilla in Connecticut but
have received no reply. It has never
occurred to me before to ask if she can
read. Some of the Southern men say that
Negroes (they never actually use that
term unless we are in class) are gifted
storytellers and only pretend to be reading.

If she visits New York and you see her,
you will have to give her my regards and
let me know how she is doing.

Love to your family,
Robert Van Vorst

EXT. A HOUSE IN MIDDLETOWN, CONNECTICUT

Two middle-aged WHITE WOMEN are talking by a

white picket fence. A YOUNG BLACK WOMAN walks
down the path, smiles, and nods toward the WHITE
WOMEN before entering the house.

> FIRST WHITE WOMAN
> They are such lovely people.

> SECOND WHITE WOMAN
> You would hardly know they were Negroes.
> Of course, you can see them. I mean, they
> don't act like Negroes, do they?

INT. A SMALL ROOM IN THE HOUSE—SAME DAY
(CONTINUOUS)

We see a figure sitting at a small table in front of the
window. From her POV we see the WHITE WOMEN
still talking at the picket fence. The camera moves
so that we see the face of PRISCILLA as she picks
up a pen and begins to write. The camera is focused
sometimes on the paper before her and sometimes on
the view from the window.

> PRISCILLA
(voice-over)
> Dear Claire,
> We are settled now here in Middletown.
> Mother is still very much upset in a noisy
> sort of way but I fear most for Father. He is

so quiet. At night he often sits by himself
in the parlor. There's no talking to him, for
he only answers in grunts. I think I know
what he is feeling. The business that we
worked so hard to build in New York was
torn down so quickly during the riots.

Claire, I miss you so much. I want to run
all the way to New York and throw my
arms around you the way we used to do.
Did you read in the papers about how our
colored soldiers are doing? I knew that
after the wonderful showing of the 54th
Massachusetts in South Carolina, they
would all do well. A woman down the
street knew the family of Colonel Shaw,
who was killed with the 54th. All the
papers speak of how brave our soldiers
have been and what a difference they are
making in this terrible war. Father says
they should have been the ones sent to
New York to calm the streets.

We do sometimes get the papers from
New York, but they arrive a week late, if
at all. That's great fun because the local
papers report the same news and you can
compare the accounts.

I wonder if you will ever visit me here. The house we have rented is quite large, and our neighbors seem to be of a decent sort. There aren't that many black people here. I never thought that sort of thing would matter, but now I actually count them.

I have received two letters from Robert, which I have not answered. It's is almost as if I have forgotten how to speak to him, which I think is crazy. I know I will answer him, but I want to say something happy and wonderful and it seems that all the happy and wonderful things ended in the summer.

I think it will be hard to maintain our friendship through letters, but in my heart I will always be your friend. I cannot wait until we are together again and sharing a laugh and a hug.

The Lord bless you and keep you, sweet Claire. The Lord make His face to shine upon you, and be gracious unto you. And give you peace. And give you peace.

Your best friend (until you find a husband),
Priscilla

EXT. THE STREETS OF NEW YORK

The camera pans the same streets at the opening of the film, but this time it stops now and again on boarded-up buildings, a few charred remains of tenements and, now and again, on doorways upon which there is placed a black wreath.

CUT TO:
LONG SHOT of the Peacock Inn. The camera zooms in slowly, pauses for a moment on the window, and then moves up to another window on the second floor.

INT. CLAIRE'S ROOM—SAME DAY (CONTINUOUS)

CLAIRE sits on the bed with a portable writing desk propped up on pillows. We hear her voice-over as she writes.

> CLAIRE
> (voice-over)
> Dear Priscilla,
> Father's changed again because of
> Mother's condition. She's developed
> a cough, which we both think needs
> watching and so we'll stay in New York
> for a while. Robert has written me two
> letters which express his excitement at
> school. I think he's equally excited to be
> away from his dreadfully stuffy parents.

We see more and more freed slaves from the
South. The poor dears come into the city
and they are so lost and uneasy. They are
also badly treated, I'm afraid. Priscilla, I am
convinced that once this war is over there
will be no more people held in chains. But I
wonder if there will be a new bondage. Will
we be trapped in our skins, forever held to
be different because we are not white? And
what wars will free us from that distinction?
Before the riots, Mr. Valentine looked upon
us as the caretakers of his property and was
pleased with us. Now he looks at us as if we
started the trouble, as if our very presence
as Negroes was the difference.

Before those four terrible days, I looked
beyond skin and saw people. But it was
our skin that made us targets, not our
hearts. I am slow to come around to being
the old Claire again, but I think she lurks
somewhere within me.

(we hear the soft sounds of "The Black Rose")
Priscilla, we can't go back again. Maybe
the three of us—you, me and Robert—
back in school were seeing things with
the eyes of children then. Perhaps our

innocence is forever gone. But sitting with
my mum and working on the quilt that you
and I started, and seeing my father get up
and push on despite his disappointment,
I think that if we can't go back, then we
should try even harder to go forward. And
I do want to go forward, to a place where
loving someone because they have a gentle
smile and a friendly hello is as easy as it
once was.

I see Maeve now and again. I think she
truly loved Liam and misses him terribly.
Life hasn't been easy for her, as it hasn't
been easy for many of the poor folks in
these streets. We share a word or two of
little importance and sometimes even a
smile. We go on with our lives. We are not
comfortable with each other, but neither
do we hate each other and that's good.

Do write Robert. I think he will love to
hear from you. But write me much, much
more, because I adore you so.

Your true friend,
and with all my love and all my heart,
Claire

The music rises as the camera pulls away from CLAIRE and continues through to the last dissolve.

EXT. THE PEACOCK INN

EXT. THE STREETS OF LOWER NEW YORK

EXT. GULLS IN SILHOUETTE OVER THE HARBOR

The End

1619: First Africans brought to North American English colonies as slaves

1775–1783: The American Revolutionary War

1776: The Declaration of Independence

1789: Despite opposition from some Americans, the newly ratified Constitution of the United States accommodates slavery. The importation of slaves is banned as of January 1, 1808, but slavery is still legal.

1827: Slavery is abolished in New York State

1845–1851: The Great Irish Famine. More than one million people die of disease and starvation in Ireland, and another million emigrate to the United States, Canada, Great Britain, and elsewhere. Many of the Irish come to New York, where, as poor immigrants, they settle in Lower Manhattan.

November 6, 1860: Abraham Lincoln is elected President. Many in the slave states see him as pushing toward abolition of slavery in the United States.

December 1860–June 1861: South Carolina secedes from the United States and is followed over the next few months by Mississippi, Florida, Alabama, Georgia, Louisiana, and Texas. Later, Arkansas, North Carolina, Tennessee, and Virginia joined the Confederacy.

February 1861: The Confederate Government is formed.

April 12, 1861: The American Civil War begins with a Confederate attack on Fort Sumter.

By January 1863: As the war rages on, mostly in the Southern states, a steady stream of blacks attach themselves to the Union Army or escape north. While few reach New York City, rumors precede them, and the city is filled with talk of thousands entering the city and competing for the few available jobs.

January 1, 1863: Lincoln issues the Emancipation Proclamation, declaring that most slaves in the areas of rebellion are free in the eyes of the federal government.

March 3, 1863: Lincoln signs the first conscription act in U.S. history, authorizing the president to draft "all

able-bodied male citizens of the United States, and
persons of foreign birth who shall have declared on oath
their intention to become citizens . . . between the ages
of twenty and forty-five years. . . ." A later section of this
law stated "That any person drafted . . . may . . . furnish
an acceptable substitute to take his place in the draft; or
he may pay . . . such a sum, not exceeding three hundred
dollars . . . for the procuration of such substitute."

July 1–3, 1863: Battle of Gettysburg. In this bloodiest
battle of the Civil War, the tide of the war turns in favor
of the Union. Lincoln decides that it would be a good
time to enact the conscription law he felt was necessary.
Several New York regiments are at Gettysburg.

July 11, 1863: First draft drawing occurs in New York
City, without incident. The provision of the draft allowing
draftees to be exempted by providing a substitute or
paying $300 was particularly galling to the poor Irish.

Monday, July 13, 1863: Second draft drawing occurs in
New York City. A crowd, led by a company of volunteer
firemen and consisting largely of poor Irish immigrants,
attacks the Provost Marshal's Office. As the violence
spreads, blacks and property became targets. The
Colored Orphan Asylum is burned down.

Tuesday, July 14, 1863: Rioters return to the streets and the violence continues. Militia ordered into New York City, including the 74th and 65th National Guard, and the vaunted Seventh Regiment, among others.

Wednesday, July 15, 1863: Draft is suspended. Violence begins to subside as militias begin to arrive and suppress rioting.

Thursday, July 16, 1863: More militias arrive. At a final confrontation near Gramercy Park, many rioters die.

April 9, 1865: General Robert E. Lee surrenders to General Ulysses S. Grant at Appomattox Court House.

April 14, 1865: President Lincoln is shot by John Wilkes Booth at Ford's Theatre and dies the next morning.

May 1865: American Civil War ends. Remaining Confederate forces surrender, and the United States is reunited.

December 6, 1865: Thirteenth Amendment to the United States Constitution is ratified, abolishing slavery.

July 9, 1868: Fourteenth Amendment is ratified, conferring citizenship on everyone born or naturalized in the United States.

February 3, 1870: The Fifteenth Amendment is ratified, conferring voting rights without regard to race, color, or previous servitude. Gender is not mentioned.

It was the bloodiest civil disturbance in American history. Four terrible days in July of 1863 that would leave hundreds dead and injured and forever change the face of New York City. How could this happen in the largest city of North America? And what would it mean for not only the participants but also for generations to follow?

The New York City Draft Riots nearly changed the course of American history. They definitely changed the hearts and minds of the people who lived and worked in our nation's busiest city. But how could so much blood run down the streets of Broadway and Fifth Avenue when the real conflict, the Civil War, was being fought hundreds of miles away?

There is what we study as "history," and then there is the history behind that history, which we must know to understand what happened. The causes of the New York

City Draft Riots begin in 1619, when the first Africans were brought across the Atlantic as slaves. These unfortunates, captured along the West Coast of Africa, worked in the cotton fields of Georgia and Alabama, in the rice paddies of South Carolina, and in the tobacco fields of Virginia and Kentucky. But they also worked in the Dutch colony of New Amsterdam. They built fortifications and houses; they cleared lands. Some managed to earn, or were given, their freedom. Others languished in slavery until their deaths. In 1991 a construction crew found more than four hundred graves of African Americans on Elk Street in Manhattan. That site is now known as the African Burial Ground.

While slavery was primarily a Southern institution, the slave trade and its products offered profits to businesspeople throughout the land, even in New York.

Blacks, free and slave, worked in New York City in many capacities before the Civil War. Some became very successful, while others lived the demeaning life typical of the lowest economic groups. Slavery was not popular in New York, and the state ended it completely in 1827. In that same year, John B. Russwurm and the Reverend Samuel Cornish, two black New York City residents, produced *Freedom's Journal*, the first newspaper published by African Americans in the United States. Black schools were opened and blacks began to run their own businesses.

By the 1850s most of the blacks in New York were not doing that well, but they were a lot better off than their brothers in the South, who, enslaved for life, had little chance for a brighter future.

Enter into this precarious economic situation an immigrant population from Europe. The Great Famine in Ireland alone caused a million deaths from disease and starvation. That many more were forced into emigration. Thousands of the Irish soon found themselves in New York City, desperately trying to compete for the few jobs available. They, like some of their black neighbors, lived in miserable conditions. The Five Points region of New York, where many of the Irish poor lived, was a dangerous and unforgiving area where people died easily and hope was scarce.

The Civil War brought a new perspective to the inhabitants of Lower Manhattan. For the blacks it meant a chance that their brothers and sisters in the South might soon be free. But for the Irish it meant that a newly freed population would now be competing for the same jobs that they so desperately longed for.

President Abraham Lincoln wanted more soldiers to fight for the Union. In March 1863, Congress gave him the authority to call a draft. Despite the Union Army's need for more men, Lincoln was hesitant because of the unpopularity of the war. But in the beginning of July 1863, Union forces turned back a determined Confederate attack in a place called Gettysburg. This, Lincoln figured, was a safe time to use the draft.

The Irish immigrants in New York City had already

been bombarded with rumors of blacks ready to enter the city and take away their jobs. Despite Lincoln's statements that the war was about preserving the Union, the Irish felt as if they were being asked to risk their lives simply to free the slaves who would then compete against them. To make matters worse, a provision of the draft said that those drafted could either provide a substitute, or buy their way out of the draft for three hundred dollars. Few people in Five Points or similar neighborhoods had anything near that amount of money. The Irish took to the streets.

The targets of Irish rage were the rich, the newspapers that supported the war, and the blacks they saw as their competition. They vented that rage for four terrible days, chasing down and murdering blacks, burning buildings (including the Colored Orphan Asylum), and attacking anyone who looked wealthy.

Gettysburg had been the bloodiest battle of the Civil War. New York supplied the second highest number of soldiers in that battle and had sustained the most casualties. When these battle-weary warriors were called back to New York City to put down the rioters, they did it with a shocking brutality, often using automatic weapons against unarmed civilians. When the riots ended, the city was in shock.

But what about the Irish and blacks who had befriended one another and worked together? How about the families who were part Irish and part black? What would the effect be on them? How would they reconcile their differences?

The aftermath of the New York City Draft Riots would

be far reaching. Many blacks left the city, never to return. Families were broken, and many neighborhoods forever changed. What happened in New York City during that one hot week would be a precursor to American history for years to come.

President Abraham Lincoln

The neighborhood Five Points, New York City

My Dear Sir

I now make an appeal to your Sympathy and kindness in my behalf; I stand alone in the world without a friend or advisor, to render me any assistance, or aid me in any way whatever,

When Gen. McClennan took Possession of this place, I applied to him for Protection for myself and Property. I enclose my application and his answer for your perusal.

I must now tell you that my Servants have revolted against my authority. Several have left me and gone off, and others on the premises are making preparation to leave. They informed me that on yesterday the Provost Marshall, had given them Passports of Freedom and would furnish them with conveyances to take them to old Point, and from thence to New York. I do not regard the loss of them individually — but their base Ingratitude, with the Insults they have heaped upon me, is more than I have strength to bear, my frail and tottering frame, having nearly numbered Four Score Years — and now I want to ask you if there are any Laws that I can call to my aid which can protect me in my own House from the Insults of the Soldiers and Slaves.

If you will come and see me I will be most thankful and your kindness will ever be most Gratefully Remembered by yr Sincere friend

Helen M Anderson

This letter from Helen M. Anderson, a slaveholder, is being sent to Lemuel Jackson Bowden, who was serving as a Virginia senator under the auspices of the Unionist Party. Miss Anderson complains that her slaves, freed by the Union Army, are being insolent and taunting her with their preparations to go to New York.

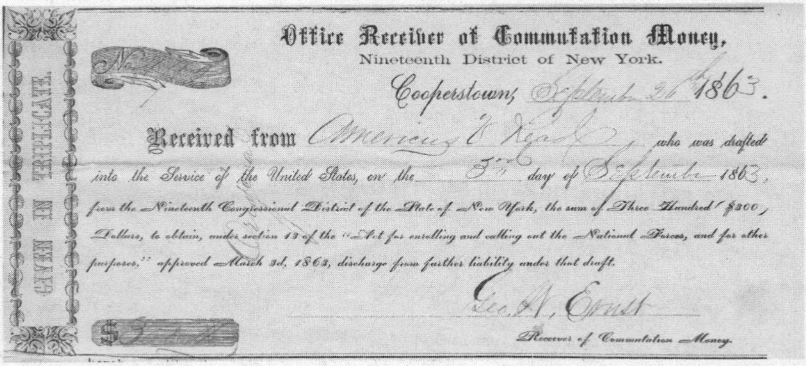

GIVEN IN TRIPLICATE.

Office Receiver of Commutation Money,
Nineteenth District of New York.

Cooperstown, September 26th 1863.

Received from Americus V. [illegible] who was drafted into the Service of the United States, on the 3rd day of September 1863, from the Nineteenth Congressional District of the State of New York, the sum of Three Hundred ($300) Dollars, to obtain, under section 13 of the "Act for enrolling and calling out the National Forces, and for other purposes," approved March 3d, 1863, discharge from further liability under that draft.

Geo. W. Ernst
Receiver of Commutation Money.

$300

Commutation certificate

Courtesy of Walter Dean Myers

Lottery wheel, used for the draft

[HANGING A NEGRO IN CLARKSON ST.]

Hanging a Negro in Clarkson Street

WOMEN - PILLAGING.

Women pillaging

Frank Leslie's Illustrated Newspaper, 7/25/1863

Colored Orphan Asylum—1860–1861

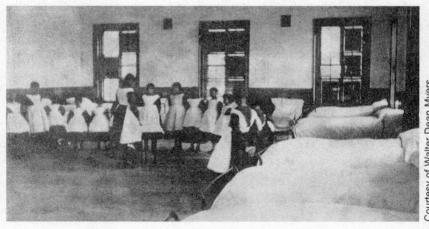

Dorm room at Colored Orphan Asylum

Harper's Weekly, 8/1/1863

BURNING OF THE COLORED ORPHAN ASYLUM

Burning of the New York Colored Orphan Asylum

ANDREWS OF VIRGINIA HARANGUING THE MOB.

John Andrews of Virginia haranguing the mob

Walt Whitman

THE LATE TUMULT IN THE CITY.

Map of the City of New York Below the Central Park, Showing the Points Attacked During the Riots of Last Week.

The Numbers in Large Figures Indicate the Wards. Those in Smaller Figures Show the Points of Attack.

Courtesy of Walter Dean Myers

Map of Manhattan from *New York Herald*—July 20, 1863

KEY TO THE MAP.

Operations on Monday.

1.—Locality of the commencement of the disturbance. Telegraph poles cut down and wires destroyed.

2.—Provost Marshal's office, where the draft for the Ninth district was being held. Three four story buildings burned.

3.—Two buildings burned.

4.—Where Police Commissioner Kennedy was beaten, and first fight with the police.

5.—Conflict with the military.

6.—Police again attacked and beaten.

7.—Bull's Head Hotel robbed and burned.

8.—Colored Orphan Asylum sacked and burned.

9.—Harlem Railroad track torn up three blocks.

10.—Armory burned and severe fighting.

11.—Two private brown stone residences pillaged and burned.

12.—Eighth district enrolling office. Entire block facing on Broadway and two houses on Twenty-eighth street burned.

13.—Seventh Avenue Arsenal frequently attacked. Severe fighting.

14.—Cottage burned.

15.—Tribune office.

16.—Gunboat off Wall street.

17.—Gunboat off the Battery for the protection of the Quartermaster's Department.

Operations on Tuesday.

18.—Crowd gathered for Tuesday's work. Company of regulars charged upon the crowd and scattered them.

19.—Another crowd congregated. Soldiers again charged and fired on the multitude and drove them.

20.—Another fight.

21.—Mayor Opdyke's house sacked.

22.—Mr. Gibbons' house sacked.

23.—Fighting all along Ninth avenue between Twentieth and Fortieth streets. Women took part.

24.—Weehawken ferry house and liquor saloon burned.

25.—Hudson River Railroad track torn up.

26.—Soap chandler's establishment destroyed.

27.—Brooks' clothing store sacked.

28.—Negro neighborhood. Negroes killed and property destroyed.

29.—Fighting nearly all day.

30.—Colonel O'Brien killed.

31.—Hotel burned.

Operations on Wednesday.

32.—Severe and bloody fighting.

33.—Gas house attacked.

34.—Negro neighborhood. Negroes driven out and York street sacked.

35.—Negro hung to a lamppost.

36.—House sacked and burned.

37.—Lumber yard burned.

38.—Three buildings occupied by colored people burned. Negro hung to a lamppost.

39.—Eighteenth precinct station house, bell tower and house of fire Engine Company No. 51 burned.

40.—Negro hung to a lamppost. Fighting with the military.

Operations on Thursday.

41.—House sacked.

42.—Lager bier saloons demolished.

43.—Thirty stores in Grand street robbed.

Operations on Friday.

44.—Mass meeting in front of the residence of Archbishop Hughes.

45.—Present headquarters of the police and military.

Key to map

Provost guard attacking the rioters

THE GREAT RIOT IN NEW YORK—SCENES ON THE 13TH AND 14TH OF JULY.—FROM SKETCHES BY OUR SPECIAL ARTISTS.

Attack on the *Tribune* office

RESUMPTION OF THE DRAFT—INSIDE THE PROVOST MARSHAL'S OFFICE, SIXTH DISTRICT—THE WHEEL GOES ROUND.

Resumption of the draft

Harper's Weekly, 9/5/1863

Two girls, the models for
Claire (standing) and Priscilla (seated)